# DRAGON MASTER

The Kaiser's One-Man Air Force
In Tsingtau, China, 1914

A non-fiction book of Military Aviation History

by

Robert E. Whittaker

Translations by

Susanne Kawatsu

Published by COMPASS BOOKS-Video-Films

DRAGON MASTER

COVER DESIGN;
"SCRATCH-BUILT" SCALE MODEL OF THE RUMPLER TAUBE
PHOTOGRAPHY AND ILLUSTRATIONS
by
Robert E. Whittaker

Cover design by computer artists Anthony & Laurel Kāshinn, Blue Rose Studio, Grafton, Wisconsin. The front cover was created by electronically merging two photographs, first in an Amiga System, and then final layout and output via the Macintosh.

Copyright © 1994 by Robert E. Whittaker

Published by COMPASS BOOKS-Video-Films.
921 Jackson Drive
Cleveland, Wisconsin 53015


Printed by
Artex Publishing Co. Inc.
Sheboygan, WI

Library of Congress Catalog Card Number: 94-70291

Hardcover ISBN 0-9639310-1-6
Paperback ISBN: 0-9639310-0-8

Printed in the United States of America

10 9 8 7 6 5 4 3 2 1

*This book is dedicated to all those people throughout the brief history of flight who have ventured bravely into earth's surrounding air and into outer space.*

# REFLECTIONS ON THE ART OF WAR

*The Dragon represents spirit and power. Both Imperial and Immortal, he is Master of the Elements....Lord of the Underworld ....Ruler of the Skies. I don't know how he rides on the wind or how he reaches the heaven...* The philosopher, Confucius (K'ung Fu-Tzu 551-459 b.c.)

*The expert commander abhors a static situation and therefor attacks cities only when there is no alternative. Sieges.... wasteful of lives, time and property, entail abdication of the initiative.*

Sun Tzu - The Art of War 506 b.c.

*An army without spies is like a man without ears or eyes.*

Chia Lin, Ancient Chinese Strategist

*In war, numbers alone confer no advantage. Do not advance relying on sheer military power. Know what is over the hill.*

Sun Tzu - The Art of War 506 b.c.

*To triumph in battle against a lesser foe and be universally acclaimed 'Expert' is not the acme of skill, for to distinguish between the sun and moon is no test of vision; To hear the thunderclap is no indication of acute hearing; To lift an autumn fog requires no great strength.*

Sun Tzu - The Art of War 506 b.c.

*A sheep that puts on a tiger skin
will never be attacked by wolves.*

Lao Wei

*To win, it is important to know your adversary...
To lose, is NOT to know oneself.*

Lao Wei

# CONTENTS

# PHOTOGRAPHS AND ILLUSTRATIONS

# INTRODUCTION

German flying aces of the First World War like Immelman, Boelche, Goering and "The Red Baron" von Richthofen received their deserved niche in military aviation history.

However there was an obscure aviator who fell through the cracks of history in a little-known Far Eastern campaign. Lieutenant Gunther Plüschow (pronounced Ploo-show) of the Imperial German Navy was pitted against nine Japanese aircraft; four Maurice-Farman sea-planes of the navy; four land M. Farmans and one Nieuport monoplane of the Army Air Corps. Plüschow was "unofficially" credited with shooting one down with his Rumpler-Taube.

The Germans, against 13-to-1 odds, defended their colonial naval base for seventy-two days against the Japanese and (token) British land-sea-air forces. The Tsingtau Siege from August to November 1914 is documented as having produced ELEVEN significant military 'FIRSTS'....SIX of which are AVIATION FIRSTS; (Two other possibles.)

1. First German warplane to crash in China during a reconnaissance flight, July 31, 1914.
2. First aerial bombs with fins dropped by the Japanese navy floatplanes on German forts and warships; September 5, 1914.

NOTE: Italian planes dropped hand grenades on Libya in 1911 and an American flyer L. Bonney dropped "explosive devices" on rebel positions for the Mexican Government in 1913. They weighed only a few pounds. On August 30, 1914 a German Taube dropped several three-kilogram explosive devices on the outskirts of Paris. All of these primitive devices exploded harmlessly.

The Japanese bombs were 14 to 45 pound artillery shells fitted with fins and pad-eyes; the first true aerodynamic aerial missiles.

Twenty-seven years later, during the attack on Pearl Harbor, the Japanese battleship Nagato's 16-inch 1,760-pound armor-piercing shells were also modified with fins and pad-eyes and dropped as bombs. Historians, both Japanese and Americans, state that one of them sank the battleship Arizona.

3. First seaplane carrier used in combat; (Japanese)
4. First air-to-sea engagement. (Japanese-German)
5. First night bombing; (Japanese)
6. First "stealth" aircraft. The Rumpler-Taube was nearly invisible at an altitude of 305 meters. (1000 feet)
7. First time Caucasian troops were commanded by Asians.
8. First capture of German territory by the Japanese in WW I.
9. First British army commander to step on German soil: WW I
10. First major loss of German colonial territory in WW I.
11. First combination of Land, Sea and Air Forces employed together in warfare.

NOTE:
A. (Possible) FIRST air-to-air combat with firearms. This "first" was disputed by an ambiguous back-dated French communique issued two months after the Tsingtau report reached Europe.
B. (Possible) FIRST anti-aircraft fire-control mechanism devised and used by the Germans against the Japanese. The rapid-fire artillery removed from the Austrian cruiser Kaiserin Elizabeth were aimed with a state-of-the-art combination of range-finders, sextants and slide rule verniers. The instruments and schematics were destroyed by the Germans.

This little-known campaign was the military "laboratory" that tested every known state-of-the-art weapon (except chemical) and awakened the sleeping monster of Japan's 20th Century militarism.

Tsingtau is noteworthy for several reasons. It has been under six flags; Manchu, Imperial Germany, Japanese / British, Republic of China and since 1949 the Peoples Republic. It was one of the ten most beautiful port cities in the world as claimed during the 1930's by Fitzpatrick the documentary film producer of the theater series "Traveltalk." It was the cleanest, most modern and healthful city in the Far East. It was and still is "THE" resort city of China. During the 1920's - 30's and between 1945 and 1949 the U.S. Navy would summer in Tsingtao and conduct maneuvers and target practice off shore in the Yellow Sea.

Militarily noteworthy:

(First) the former German colony and Naval base was an outstanding example of field fortifications as it was understood prior to the "Great War" of 1914.

(Second) Because of the comparatively small damage to the works after 72 days of siege and much of which was still standing after a lapse of 27 years. (1941 was the last year the author lived there before being interned after 'Pearl Harbor' by the Japanese.)

In many places the stencil marking, in German script, designating assignments of machine gun emplacements could still be seen. Poignant messages scratched or smeared in blood on the walls of the underground field hospitals by the wounded and dying were still visible. Others were simply "Kilroy was here" signatures.

Much of the "Big Ditch" that stretched from the Yellow Sea to Kaiochow Bay remained, also the strands of heavy barbed wire and metal posts that were not scavanged. Many of the fortifications were still intact in 1949 when the Peoples Army took over the city and dropped the "bamboo curtain". Most notable of these forts is

x

Hweichuen Point that was nearly completely intact even to the metal bunk beds, galley stoves, sinks and gun emplacements. This particular fort was a tourist attraction and a Chinese caretaker would take visitors on a paid tour. The author was very familiar with it.

Robert E. Whittaker was born in Shanghai, lived in China and Tsingtau for over 17 years and has knowledge of the siege from German veterans who returned from Japanese POW camps to live in this "piece of the Fatherland in China."

Whittaker acquired 2,993 pages of historical documents and microfilm on the siege from the archives of the United States, Germany and Japan with which to create this unique saga that took over three years.

The crowning achievement was locating Lieutenant Plüschow's SON now living in Canada. Gunter G. Plueschow has been of great help in providing documents, photos and his first hand recollections of his father and also by giving a personal critique on this book.

*******

*"My dear Robert, I would like to express my gratitude to you that you let my father come alive again with your research and with what you write about him.*

*Your description of my father and what he has done is fantastic. You write and speak as if you knew him personally."*

Gunter Guntolf Plueschow
Winnipeg, Canada
November 1993

# CLARIFICATIONS and APOLOGIES

The Chinese names in this book are spelled the way they were at the time. The German spelling of Tsingtau was later spelled Tsingtao in English and correctly pronounced (Ching-Dao) when the author lived there in the 20's and 30's. However most foreigners pronounced it "Sing-tao." The new Pinyin system makes the spelling of the city; Qingdao (Ching-Dao). Likewise the names of Peking, Nanking, Tientsin, Chefoo and others are from that era and are not spelled the same today. The German spelling of various names and locations are at times interspersed with the English spelling that the author is more familiar with and for easier reading; likewise the conversion from and to the metric system.

The derogatory name calling such as; "The Yellow Peril," "Japs," "Yellow Monkeys," "Brown Dwarfs," "Smelly Barbarians," "Brits," "Limeys," "Yanks," "Square-heads," "Krauts," "Chinks," "Coolies" and "Pigtails," were used in written statements, diaries and newspaper reports at the time and have been included as historical fact and not to demean the various nationalities and races.

Instead of tedious footnotes and documentation sources indicated by reference numbers at the end of each page, chapter or book, the author has chosen to incorporate as many as possible within the text for continuity and easier reading. The nearly 3000 pages of reference material would in itself be several books if printed. However, nine major archival sources have been listed along with a bibilography and a list of books for further reading.

So instead of creating a tome of historic proportions useful only to libaries, archives and military theoreticians this author has endeavored to write in a documentary style for wider popular appeal.

There are actual quotes from official documents and newspaper clippings as well as anecdotal stories and personal accounts told by those involved in their own words, albeit translated into English.

The general readership will not only be caught up in this little-known military campaign, but through the eyes of a heroic pioneer aviator will be on an Oriental travelogue.

The writer has tried not to be biased, but since most of the conflict is told through the eyes of the defenders, it probably would seem to be slanted favorably towards the Germans. That was not the intention. In all fairness they deserved the facts.

There will be great bravery and great blunders on both sides. Caught in the middle are the long-suffering Chinese; their land occupied by "Foreign Devils" from three nations; their country devasted by a foreign war.

There will be poignant vignettes of heroism and humorous anecdotes all related within the stage backdrop of a vicious siege. Woven within this literary tapestry are the sights, smells and sounds of old China as experienced by the Kaiser's One-Man Air Force... The Dragon Master of Tsingtau.

---

"It is always interesting to see accounts of how fledgling air services learned to flex their muscles and experiment with their equipment before the larger war began. Robert Whittaker's account of a German pilot flying a single Rumpler Taube in the defense of the German colony at Tsingtau is one of the most interesting and moving of them all. He describes the operation of the aeroplane among the surroundings and the culture of the Chinese people, and opens a window onto the background of much of the air warfare which too many of us take for granted. A wonderful piece of work, handsomely illustrated."

Leonard E. Opdycke, WWI AEROPLANES, INC.

Kemp Tolley, a Naval Historian has been helpful with suggestions and inputs. He is the author of such non-fiction books as Yangtze Patrol, Cruise of the Lanikai, and Caviar and Commissars: The Experiences of a U.S. Naval Officer in Stalin's Russia, all published by the Naval Institute Press. After reading the manuscript of "The Dragon Master" he writes:

"It is <u>most</u> interesting and amusing and a piece of history that certainly needed doing. It is especially interesting to assess the capabilities of the Germans and the Japanese and to what extent it was carried on in the practices of the two militaries. Clearly, the Germans excelled on the ground - while the Japanese early on recognized the future of aircraft. Certainly these characteristics were evident in WW II, both strategically and tactically. And of course the Japanese carried it to its' ultimate in the Kamikaze."

Kemp Tolley
Rear Admiral, USN (Ret)
Monkton, Maryland
April 1993

# FOREWORD
by
Carl V. Ragsdale,
Captain, USNR (Ret)

"The vivid descriptions and flavor of this little-known historical account of World War One in China will be fascinating to military and civilian readers and "Old China Hands." I am all three.

Having served as the Western Pacific Fleet Camera Officer in Tsingtao from 1946 to 1947, I was able to visually reminisce what it must have been like some 32 years previously in 1914 through the author's well researched and detailed descriptions of both the city and the siege. Most of the buildings, pensions, hotels, streets and boulevards and the race course, (formerly the air-field) were still intact along with the German fortifications that were even then, tourist attractions. This remarkable story is all the more appealing, being set amidst the beautiful and exotic Far Eastern seaport of Tsingtao.

I have known Bob Whittaker since 1965 and we have swapped "sea-stories" and pictures of his hometown Tsingtao, as well as making films together all over the world.

As an award-winning motion picture Producer/Director of military and documentary films, that included an Academy Award, and being familiar with Tsingtao, I can truly recommend this interesting and well documented saga of military and aviation history."

*Carl V Ragsdale*

Signed: Carl V. Ragsdale

# Acknowledgments

Many people have inspired this book, and I wish to thank them all. If I miss any, and I'm sure I shall, I apologize.

The German veteran Fred Bischof who was living in Tsingtao in the 1930's and who would recount the Siege to eager ears.

The Chinese caretaker (who's name escapes me) at the Hweichuen Fort who would guide me through the deep underground labyrinths and who would relate his experiences of the Japanese assault still fresh in his memory after two dozen years.

Manfred Zimmermann the ex "Oberleutnant" who was born in Tsingtau, fought there, was captured there and in the 1940's died there.

Karl Volchek, who's German mother was one of the nurses and who married a "White Russian".

My mother, Evelyn Larsen Whittaker, the principal of the Tsingtao American School as well as an Associated Press Correspondent who inspired me to write and be published at the age of fourteen.

I also wish to thank those who have helped me with research and other work;

* Katherine Reynolds and Sondra Bierre; Hoover Institution Archives, Stanford, CA
* Patty M. Maddocks; United States Naval Institute, Annapolis,
* Richard A. von Doehnhoff; National Archives, Washington, DC
* Irina Renz; Library of Contempory History, Stuttgart, Germany
* Dr. Fleischer; Bundesarchiv-Militararchiv, Freiburg, Germany
* Dennis Park; Librarian, Experimental Aircraft Association Foundation Boeing Aeronautical Library, Oshkosh, Wisconsin.

* Arthur H. Sanfelici; Editor of the magazine "Aviation" who responded favorably to my query for an article on the "Kaiser's One-Man Air Force (in China)". The resulting 30 months of research provided enough material for this book.

* Neal Hatayama, Hawaii State Library, Honolulu, HI

* Carrel Morgan, Wayne, NJ (son of Doctors Lorenzo and Ruth Morgan, Haichow, China.)

* Nancy Allman Burnham, Paris, France, formerly of Tsingtao.

* Leonard Opdycke, Publisher, World War I Aeroplanes, Inc. Poughkeepsie, NY.

* Keith W. Fredericks, President, Pohlman Studios, Inc. Milwaukee, WI

* Les Zielinski, Artex Publishing, Inc., Sheboygan, WI

* To Laurel & Anthony Kashinn of the Blue Rose Studio, Grafton, Wisconsin, thank you for your creative computer pictures & cover.

* To my wife Nancy Oldenburg-Whittaker for her excellent suggestions and painstaking proof-reading... many thanks.

* And to Professor Susanne Kawatsu, who proficiently teaches several languages, I am most indebted for her translations.

* Special thanks must be given to Gunter G. Plueschow II and his wife Rosemarie, not only for their generous help, but also their warm and friendly hospitality during my research.

# PROLOGUE

LONDON DAILY MAIL 4, July 1915
EXTRA LATE WAR EDITION
HUNT FOR ESCAPED GERMAN
High-Pitched Voice as a Clue.

Scotland Yard last night issued the following amended description of Gunther Plüschow, one of the German prisoners who escaped from Donington Hall, Leicestershire, on Monday:
Height 5 ft. 5 1/2 in, weight 135 lb; complexion fair, hair blond, eyes blue, and tattoo marks; Chinese dragon on left arm.

As already stated in the "Daily Chronicle", Plüschow's companion, Trefftz, was recaptured on Monday evening at Millwall Docks. Both men are Naval Officers. An earlier description stated that Plüschow is 29 years old. His voice is high-pitched.

He is particularly smart and dapper in appearance, has very good teeth, which he shows somewhat prominently when talking or smiling, is "very English in manner," and knows this country well. He also knows Japan well. He is quick and alert, both mentally and physically, and speaks French and English fluently and accurately. He was dressed in a grey lounge suit or grey and yellow mixture suit.

———

# EXTRA LATE WAR EDITION

## HUNT FOR ESCAPED GERMAN,

### HIGH - PITCHED VOICE AS A CLUE.

Scotland Yard last night issued the following amended description of Gunther Pluschow, one of the two German prisoners who escaped from Donington Hall, Leicestershire, on Monday :—

Height, 5ft. 8½in.; weight, 135lb.; complexion, fair; hair, blonde; eyes, blue; and tattoo marks, Chinese dragon on left arm.

As already stated in "The Daily Chronicle," Pluschow's companion, Trepplts, was recaptured on Monday evening at Millwall Docks. Both men are naval officers. An earlier description stated that Pluschow is 29 years old. His voice is high-pitched.

He is particularly smart and dapper in appearance, has very good teeth, which he shows somewhat prominently when talking or smiling; is "very English in manner," and knows this country well. He also knows Japan well. He is quick and alert, both mentally and physically, and speaks French and English fluently and accurately. He was dressed in a grey lounge suit or grey and yellow mixture suit.

LONDON DAILY MAIL   11 July 1915
PLÜSCHOW STILL FREE

---

## THE CHINESE DRAGON CLUE

Gunther Plüschow, the German naval lieutenant, fugitive from Donington Hall, has now been at large seven days. The Chinese dragon tattooed on his left arm while on service in the East should, however, betray his identity.

# DRAGON MASTER

## GUNTHER PLÜSCHOW

WW I Pilot's badge

# CHAPTER 1

## ARRIVAL AT TSINGTAU
### June 1914

The two European men looked eagerly out the windows of first class as the train slowly entered the station. On the large brick building facade the name of the city was painted in Chinese characters and German script; Tsinanfu, Capital of Schantung Province. The tallest of the two passengers, studied his guide book and noted that Schantung means "Mountains East" and is said to be China's "Holy Land." To the right he could see the peaks of Tai Shan forty kilometers (25 miles) to the south east. The six thousand foot holy mountain is the burial place and shrine of Confucius the revered Chinese sage who lived 551-459 b.c.

As the train would continue south to Nanking and Shanghai, the two travellers had to change trains here for the final ten hour leg of their journey to the port of Tsingtau. They were directed by a German rail official to their car emblazoned with the crest of the Imperial Eagle and were elated to hear their mother tongue spoken to them for the first time since they left Berlin. It was early June 1914. The exact date was not recorded.

The journey of over six thousand six hundred miles had taken them nearly fifteen days on Russia's trans-Siberian railroad. They travelled across the monotonous steppes and deserts to Harbin, and Mukden in Manchuria, then boarded a train of the Republic of China that took them through Peking, Tientsin and now to Tsinanfu.

As they settled in the modern rail car none of the other passengers paid much attention to them. They were a mixture of Orientals and Europeans; businessmen and diplomats, some with

1

families on vacation from Tientsin and Peking. Several German naval officers on leave, wearing baggy white summer uniforms, settled into their seats. The shorter of the two travellers from Berlin went into the lavatory with his hand baggage. When he reappeared Gunther Plüschow was freshly shaven, his blonde hair combed back and parted in the middle, and he was dressed in the immaculate uniform of a Lieutenant in the German Navy's Flying Corps. He was wearing the pilot's badge. The summer heat was apparently ignored by the aviator in his dapper dress blues.

The other man, Lieutenant Friedreich Muellerskowski, also an aviator, but assigned to the III Seebatalion (Marines), was peeved that his uniform was packed away in his trunk and not accessible. He was taller than Plüschow, who was slim and of average height, but in his travel-worn civilian clothes Muellerskowski's height and bearing was not impressive. There had been some professional rivalry between the two ever since they started the trip. Perhaps because Plüschow was a well known celebrity to fellow airmen. He, together with another German flyer, had just broken the World's altitude flying record and he also looked different. Most of the German military men of that era, especially officers, had bushy handle-bar moustaches. Plüschow was clean shaven which made him look younger than his late twenties.

The insignia of an airman had never been seen in this part of the world. It was even a rarity in Germany during those early years of fledgling flyers. The bolder of the German officers of equal or higher rank immediately started a conversation with the newcomers, directed primarily at Plüschow. The other passengers listened intently. First they wanted recent first hand news of the Fatherland. Then they asked questions:

"Where is your home city?"

"How did you get into the Flying Corps?"

"Where did you learn to fly?"

"How did you manage such a wonderful assignment to Tsingtau?"

"Where is your aeroplane?"

"What is that badge and decoration?"

Plüschow answered every question, leaving the last one to be more thoroughly detailed.

"It was in August of 1913 when I returned to my hometown Schwerin. (It is in the north just east of Hamburg) I had been in England studying and the exploring the rich art treasures, learning the language, vacationing and visiting the country.

For the past one and a half years I was an Inspection Officer at the Navy Training Center, but I always wanted to fly."

There have been some reports hinting that Plüschow, who spoke fluent English and French, was on an espionage mission for the Germans in 1913.

Plüschow continued:

"My uncle had some influence and knew of my strong desire to become a flyer. When he came to meet me, he said only three words, "Congratulations...Navy Pilot!" I then learned that after training was completed, my assignment was to be Tsingtau, China. The first of January 1914 finally came, and I was in my beloved Berlin. I felt the restlessness! On January 2nd I reported to Johannisthal and expected to start my flight training immediately. But it had begun to snow and the whole aeroport was buried under a deep winter blanket. To fly was impossible.

For weeks I reported every day but could only study the aeroplanes inside the hangers, sit in the cockpits and operate the controls. Most were Rumpler-Taubes, the plane I would learn in. To wait, wait and wait again! It seemed that eighty percent of flying is waiting and being ready.

Finally on February 1, the weather cleared. My teacher was Werner Wieting and with him I sat elated in the Taube and ascended for the first time into the wonderful cold winter air. I soon realized I was gifted and had the feel for aviation. After the third day of flight training, I was proud when my instructor let me fly alone.

Two days later, after flying all by myself, instructor Wieting came to me and said: "Flying-Officer Plüschow would you like to take your flying examination now? That would be a nice record! For you and for me."

Minutes later I climbed in my machine and took off and made the prescribed curves and turns, landings and take offs with my little "Dove."

It was elating to fly in the clear winter sky. After I performed the last test landing perfectly, my instructor proudly shook my hand and congratulated me. I felt very good. It had taken five days from the start of my flying lessons to being qualified for a pilot's certificate. They told me no one else had done it in less time, for most it took longer."

Lt. Plüschow displayed his pilot's insignia with pride and pointed out the engraved Taube aircraft flying above a country scene enclosed within a wreath and topped with the Kaiser's crown. He next described what the decoration on his chest was for. There was only one other in existence. As Muellerkowski had heard this account many times during the trip, he excused himself to go clean up and shave before the midday meal.

Plüschow:

"After only a few weeks of flying, I was proud to have been given a special assignment. Herr E.C. Rumpler the famous aeroplane engineer had developed a new Taube

4

monoplane with a 100 horsepower engine which was particularly well suited for climbing to high altitudes. It was now a matter of German pride to break the world's altitude record of 5300 meters held by a Frenchman in a Bleriot. The famous pilot Otto Linnekogel would steer the plane. He asked me to fly along as observer and 2nd pilot.

On the last days of February, we started for our first test flight. We were heavily clothed for protection against the terrible cold. There was a crowd of flyers and mechanics watching us with envy as the bird lifted itself from the ground as light as a dragon-fly, after a short take-off. I observed the altitude gage, and after only 15 minutes, 2000 meters were reached, an exceptional achievement. But from then on we climbed slowly. The air became very cold and turbulent. We were tossed about like a feather in powerful air pockets. After an hour, we finally reached 4000 meters. But then the engine started to falter and soon stopped abruptly. We glided in spirals (wide tail-spins) toward the ground at high speed, but were able to level off and land safely on the airfield. The cold had been too great. The engine had simply frozen."

Ordinary crude lubricating oil of the day congealed in the extreme cold of high altitude. It was verified from Linnegogel and Plüschow's high altitude tests and others that castor oil had to be employed to lubricate the engines. The fumes, of course, traveled directly from the engine to the pilots in their open cockpits. Breathing such fumes for an hour or so was found to have the same effect upon the human body as would a straight dose of three or four spoonfuls of the strong laxative. This almost humorous peril of early flying was not reported in the diaries of the pilots and was avoided being mentioned in all known histories and documentation of high altitude flights and aerial combat of the time. The author Quentin Reynolds briefly touched on the subject in his World War I book "They Fought For The Sky".

It was vaguely hinted at in Plüschow's memoirs. He wrote that he had "acquired a fondness for blackberry brandy", and that "it kept him warm" at high altitudes. That was the standard antidote that was used to help alleviate the embarrassing problem of diarrhea then and now.

The Lieutenant now had the entire car of the train listening intently.

"Improvements were made with the engine and oil. After a few days we commenced the same test again. This time we had better luck. Safely and steadily we gained altitude. 4000 meters, 4200, 4500. The record of the last flight had been broken. The cold was almost unbearable. There was nothing to shield our heads from the wind, except our helmets and goggles. Our faces nearly froze. Even the thickest fur could not have protected us. The engine was still running. 4800, 4900 meters! Only 400 meters left to reach our goal. But as under a magic spell, the airplane refused to climb one meter higher. The fuel was almost gone, and again the engine suddenly coughed and died at a height of 4900 meters. Without a single drop of benzin we reached the ground almost frozen to death. We had not broken the world's record, but it was a respectable success. The German altitude record was won. This success spurred us to reach the final goal.

At the beginning of March, the weather was finally good enough to try again. Wrapped in even thicker furs, equipped with thermometers and a sealed barograph to document the altitude, but without oxygen equipment, we took off on our third attempt. The first altitude levels were reached without problems. On the way up we circled a giant Zeppelin and waved to each other. After an hour of struggling to ascend, we reached 4800 meters, then came 4900 meters. My altitude meter, built in the cockpit soon showed 5000. The engine and propeller hummed its regular song. Linnekogel circled calmly and safely. The thermometer showed minus 35 degrees Celsius (-30 F), but we didn't pay attention to the cold. The thin air became a problem. We felt tired, and our lungs struggled in short stinging breaths. Each movement was difficult and great effort had to be expended.

But we could still admire the view. Berlin was far below. The buildings looked like doll houses with puffy balls of cotton floating above them. After what seemed like a long time and we seemed to be still climbing, I was disappointed when my altitude meter only showed 5000 meters. Linnekogel started to give me signs to look for the airport. No! That would never do. Angrily, I shook Linnekogel who was sitting in front of me and held my five fingers under his nose and pointed my other hand upwards. Higher, higher! We were only at 5000 meters! He couldn't hear me.

Linnekogel only laughed, took my hand, shook it and signaled twice five with his other hand. I thought he was crazy from lack of oxygen and cold. Surely so because Linnekogel shut off the engine and flew swiftly down towards the airport of Johannisthal. Sixteen minutes later we landed. Spectators crowded around the Taube when they saw the crazy man waving his arms and laughing wildly.

We had succeeded! Linnekogel was right: The world's record of 5300 meters had been broken! My altitude meter had frozen at 5000 meters, positioned as it was further back from the heat of the engine. But the barograph in the front cockpit still functioned and officially registered the record of 5,500 meters (18,045 ft). It had only taken one hour and 45 minutes to do so."

Even though the midday meal was being served in the adjoining dining car, not one passenger left until Plüschow had finished his account. Travelling east all afternoon the train made stops at several cities and towns. That's why it took 10 hours to complete 350 kilometers (250 miles). The country for the most part was made up of rolling bare hills whose tops were sometimes crowned by boulders and rugged rock formations. Flourishing farm lands were dotted with tiny mud villages and towns centuries old. Ravines and "Nullahs" creased the sides of the mountains like wrinkles in the faces of ancient farmers that worked the land.

The roofs of grey half-round slate shingles were up-swung at the corners, believed "to impale the demons as they slid down." The one and two storied houses were surrounded by moats and walls within which towered ancient ginkgo trees. The orchards of peach, apples, plums and persimmons were in full bloom. This tapestry of the Shantung countryside was interspersed by streams, dry river beds and dirt roads. On the latter travelled a strange assortment of traffic; Two wheeled pony carts piled high with produce; bicycles; sedan chairs; rickshaws; an occasional motor car or truck honking its horn continuously; and the unique northern Chinese wheelbarrow. This vehicle had an enormous single wooden wheel in the center and could carry 6 people, three seated backs against each side of the wheel and drawn by a man or boy and guided and balanced from behind by another.

Most of the passengers had seen all this before and were not interested in sightseeing. Plüschow was sleeping. Only Muellerkowski seemed fascinated. He intently studied the guide book on the Orient, particularly on Tsingtau.

Until 1891 Tsingtau had no history. At that time the Imperial Chinese Government decided that Kiaochow Bay was a strategic part of the Shantung Coast and established a garrison of a few thousand men there. The fishing village was named Tsing-tau "Green Island" after it's namesake in the bay.

In 1897 two German missionaries were murdered in the interior of Shantung Province. Whether this was perpetrated by political dissidents, bandits or religious fanatics was never determined. The Germans welcomed the excuse to thwart the British colonial expansion in China which had previously acquired Hong Kong in the south and Wei-Hai-Wei on the Shantung north coast. In typical gunboat diplomacy of the times, but with utmost swiftness, the German Emperor, Wilhelm II dispatched Admiral Otto von Diedrichs with three German warships, *the Comoran, the Princess Wilhelmine* and the flagship *Kaiser.* On November 13, 1897 they fired a few shots at the Yamen (police station), landed a contingent of 600 marines, ran up the German ensign as the ship's cannon gave a twenty-one gun salute and took possession of the village. The few Chinese troops fled. There was no bloodshed.

In March 1898, the Manchu government had no other choice but sign a treaty leasing Tsingtau and a district around it of some 500 square kilometers together with the deep-water bay of Kiaochow and the islands off the coast to Imperial Germany. The term of the lease was 99 years; the purpose, "for the repairing and equipping ships; for storing of materials and supplies for the same, and for all other furnishings belonging thereto."

The treaty also authorized the construction of a railway, granted concessions for mining within a thirty li (nine mile) zone along the railway, and provided for the establishment of fortifications for the protection of the harbor.

In March, 1904 the harbor was completed. On the circular mole surrounding it were workshops accommodating 2,000 men. All types of ship repairs were possible and small steamers could be built and lifted by an enormous 160 ton crane. There was also a 16,000 ton floating dry dock installed, the largest in Asia, one of the largest and finest in the world. On June 1, 1904 the 395 kilometer railway between Tsingtau to Tsinanfu was open to traffic operated for the most part by

9

the Germans.

The former fishing village was soon transformed into a modern commercial port and naval bastion by the influx of the German navy, marines and civilian colonists. Their engineers laid out the city according to the most current European designs of the early Twentieth century.

They began with a modern sewer and water system to guarantee Tsingtau the healthiest conditions in all of Asia. Under German supervision, thousands of Chinese coolies constructed wide macadamized streets, tree-lined promenades and an excellent electrical system. The brick, stone and red slate-roofed buildings, schools, churches, hospitals, hotels, residences, beer gardens and cafes, including a fine German brewery, looked like miniature transplants of the "Fatherland." The harbor and land approaches were heavily fortified albeit with older model cannons. Hundreds of thousands of traditional German trees, pine, oak, beech, alders and birch, were imported from the Fatherland and carefully planted. The acacia trees, from German East Africa bearing large sharp thorns, were especially useful to camouflage and protect the fortifications. They also grew rapidly.

After the last stop at the village of Tschau t'sun, the train crossed the bridge over the Paischa-ho (White-Sand River) into German territory. The smell of manure and human fertilizer prevalent in the farmlands now gave way to the odor of the sea and shore. To the right stretched the bay of Kiaochow and the Tsingtau harbor. Scores of sampans fishing or carrying goods were seen sailing or being yulaoed over the smooth water like black water bugs. Dozens of merchant ships from several nations were anchored in the bay awaiting berths at the piers. With their cargo booms rigged, they looked like giant beatles floating upside down, with legs in the air.

The German battle cruisers, *Scharnhorst, Gneisenau* and *Emden* were docked at the pier along with a British warship. On June 12th, Vice-Admiral Thomas M. Jerram, the British commander-in-chief of their China squadron had made an inopportune courtesy visit. The freshly painted British heavy cruiser H.M.S. *Minotaur*, flying the Admiral's colors was decorated fore and aft with bright signal flags and bunting, the crew in spotless uniforms. She was berthed next to the *Scharnhorst* and across from the *Gneisenau*. The German warships, in contrast, were sea-worn and rusty having recently returned from their Pacific patrol.

As the train neared the city, the red and orange tiled roofs of the houses and buildings came into view looking like colorful berries amongst the bright green trees of the hills. The grape-like clusters of white blossoms on the Acacia trees looked like patches of snow. The Chinese style houses changed into modern European dwellings, truly a "Piece of the Fatherland in China."

In mid-summer of 1914 over 100 new houses and buildings were under construction. The colonial Germans provided a constant proof of their industriousness. With Tsingtau as their headquarters, the mining companies, banking firms, railroad engineers, merchants and businessmen spread throughout north China even to the Russian border. The British influence while strong in Hong Kong and south China was being reduced up north by the Germans. At the time only two strong powers were in the area; Japan and Germany.

Plüschow:
"The train slowly entered the main station of Tsingtau. Finally, after six years, I saw Tsingtau again. Again, I was on German soil, in a German city in the Far East."

In October 1906 Plüschow had travelled to the Far East aboard the Imperial mail ship *Prinz Regent Luitpold*. He was a cadet-officer in the Imperial German navy and assigned to the armored cruiser *Bismarck*, berthed at Tsingtau. It was here that he had obtained the dragon tattoo. The tail started at his left shoulder and the head at the forearm and as he later told his son "it took over two thousand needle

11

pricks" to create the dragon that was mostly green, a little blue and red. Later he would be named the Dragon Master, and the tattoo would serve him in good stead as an identity passport.

Plüschow also spent several years travelling the Orient aboard the schoolship *Sthoch*. Yearly the ship would make a voyage to the South Seas, East Indies, Siam and then back to China. He was aboard the *Bismarck* when it surveyed Tsushima Strait, between Japan and Korea, where the Japanese warships sank the Russian fleet during the Russo-Jap war of 1904-05. The German warship also paid a "courtesy" call at Dairen/Port Arthur, the former Russian naval fortress. It was actually to study Japanese naval tactics and possibly learn about their current defenses.

The spectacular Japanese victory over the Russians had amazed the European powers including the United States. The latter had no further aspirations of colonial footholds in Asia after acquiring the Philippines from Spain in 1898. Instead America came into the Pacific and the Far East as a business trading power. Russia's humiliation and Japan's challenging role was igniting both nationalism and militarism in Asia especially that of Japan. Germany clearly saw the vulnerability of it's Tsingtau colony.

Plüschow returned to Germany aboard the merchant ship *Lutzow* in 1910 to become a navy lieutenant. Only two years later the Manchu government, described as a "decayed log eaten within by termites and covered with silk brocade", crumbled under Sun Yat Sen's popular revolution. The Ching Dynasty ended, and the Chinese Republic was born on November 11, 1911.

# CHAPTER 2

## FIRST FLIGHT; DISASTER

The secondary train depot was in Tapautau, the Chinese quarter adjacent to Tsingtau that bordered the native junk harbor. The train would only stop here for a few moments to disconnect and let off the second and third class passengers. These were mostly Chinese peasants and coolie workers.

The Chinese shops that could be seen from the train were a combination of east and west. Open to the sidewalk they exhibited a strange alfresco style of shopping. The main food market, was merely small shops grouped together under a single roof and provided a unique diversity of sights, sounds and smells. Glazed duck and other prepared fowl hung by their necks and feet along with dried fish of many varieties. Large coffin-like wood troughs contained live fish to be chosen by the shopper. Pigs and chickens noisily objected to their cramped wicker baskets. Nondescript pieces of meat abuzzing with flies were displayed in the racks of the butcher stores. The better butchers who catered to Europeans kept the meat and flies under glass. Colorful vegetables and fruit and grain were in great abundance. The bakeries were filled with various breads and pastries. North China doesn't grow rice so more grain and noodles are eaten. Shoppers were Chinese as well as Europeans with their servants.

The train started again and slowly moved to the main station only a kilometer distant. Here the stores looked more European. The Chinese characters designating the name of the shop would be supplemented with a German hand-scripted caption, usually quite incongruous, possibly made up by a German with a curious sense of humor. A cobbler was named Mist Schuster, "Manure Boot-maker"; And the shoe store next to him was "Manure no. 2." The barber was Schaum-Kopf, "Bubble-head;" A tailor was "Rooster" because of his raucous laughter. And so it went, a strange, yet humorous mingling of the east and west, a piece of Europe....a Teutonic foothold built here in China through the organized design and determined effort of the Germans.

The Platz around the station was thronged with a variety of visitors and transportation. Rickshaws, drawn by stalwart Shangtungese were the main mode, horse carriages next. European women, who were in a few open touring automobiles, shaded the late afternoon sun with parasols. A German and a Chinese policeman directed traffic.

The two aviators were met at the train by a non-commissioned officer who got a teen age coolie boy and a carriage driver to help with the baggage.

Since the revolution, in order to give the Chinese government a "save face" participation in the running of the German colony, Customs houses had been set up at both the docks and the railway station. The main Customs office at dockside was more impressive than the mere shack at the station. The formalities of passing through Customs meant only a laconic wave and a toothy grin from the Chinese official with a long black pigtail and a pair of metal rimmed spectacles made of plain window glass just for "face."

The prime method of transportation, one step better than the rickshaws, were the European style carriages, with the driver up front and seats for four in the rear with trunks piled up behind. It was pulled by two small Mongolian horses hardly larger than ponies. These more elegant "two-horse power" carriages were used to carry larger loads of luggage. However, most of the others, were only "one-horse wagons."

The first stop, at Plüschow's insistence, was the Post and Telegraph office. It was an impressive three story building made of brick. Ornate woodwork around the windows gave it the look of a transplant from Bavaria. At the front peak by the sharply slanting red tile roof, was the crest of the Imperial German eagle. The German flag extended from a pole over the front door and from a flagpole on the roof between the two pyramid spires which rose another two stories. Only the rickshaws waiting at the curb could indicate that it was not a modern government building in Berlin. NOTE PHOTO.

After the two flyers posted letters to Germany, having received none, they doubled back on the sightseeing tour of the city on the way to the officer's "haus". They rode through streets marked in Chinese characters as well as in German script; Tsimo, Kiautschou, Kaumi, Haipo, Schantung and Litsun. Other street names included Berliner, Prinz Heinrich, Hohenzollern-strasse, Bremer, Albert, Kronprinzen, Buelow-strasse, etc.. Truly a piece of transplanted Europe except for the throngs of bicycles, rickshaws and carts drawn by coolie power.

Most of the Chinese men had long pigtails hanging down their backs. Muellerkowski commented about this odd custom to Plüschow, and the non-commissioned officer, not knowing that Plüschow had previously visited Asia, took it upon himself to explain facts that were probably not in the guide book.

"The former Manchus who ruled China since 1644 believed that the horse is a slave... a beast of burden. They forced the conquered Chinese to wear a single long strand of braided hair... a subservient sign of a horse's tail. It singled out the Manchus who had short hair. It used to be a capital offense for a Chinaman not to have his shaved forehead and queue. Only convicted criminals had their heads completely shaven. After the revolution the pigtails were no longer required or even tolerated in China. It was considered counter-revolutionary to wear one. But customs die hard after hundreds of years. Here under German authority the old ways have not changed."

This German student of Chinese history had taught Plüschow something he wasn't aware of, but he kept this fact to himself. He was glad that Muellerkowski let the non-com reply instead of expecting him to respond.

Friedrich street was an impressive boulevard of macadam some forty feet wide lined with sidewalks and young trees. A parade of twelve men abreast could easily fit on the street even with rickshaws at the curb on either side. Here there were more Europeans. As they passed the sidewalk cafes and beer gardens, Plüschow's blue dress uniform commanded attention and became the topic of conversation with the evening patrons who were drinking and eating. Muellerkowski still wore his civilian clothes.

One such establishment was Arnold Bauman Hotel Metropole and "Warenhause" a department store. Plüschow remembered it. The two story building had eight rooms upstairs; the store and lobby downstairs. Next to it was a restaurant-pension with a beer garden in front behind a two meter high metal fence. On the second floor were eight rooms for "ladies of the night" who summered here. On the third floor lived the owner and his wife, who also was the proprietress and head chef. She had 4 servants.

Another impressive boulevard named Bismarck led them south to the bay entrance. The street ended at Kaiser Wilhelm strasse that ran along Tsingtau bay and swimming Beach Number Two. The carriage slowed for the newcomers to take in the view as it turned left. There was a long pier used for promenading and sightseeing that jutted out towards Tsingtau's namesake, Green Island, renamed Arkona by the Germans. At it's peak was a white lighthouse. To the right some 800 meters away on a spit of land was the German-Chinese high school. (SEE PHOTO) The even larger college was up near Signal Hill beyond the Government buildings.

The boulevard was impressive. Wider than the others it had a promenade with benches and trees every 15 meters or so. A metal balustrade set in heavy cement posts stretched the length of the granite wall that slanted above the beach. A hedge separated the pedestrians from the traffic. Tall electric light globes were suspended in metal reinforced cement poles. Along this beautiful thoroughfare was the

Central Hotel, Hotel Prinz Heinrich next to the prominent Deutsch-Asiatische Bank, several pensions, beer gardens, cafes and cabarets. Soon they passed Government Haus; a massive four story granite building with a wide stretch of dual roadway circling to the main entrance. Between the driveways were lawns, flower gardens, trees and walkways. Not even Shanghai or HongKong were as impressive as the German colony of Tsingtau, certainly not for climate or cleanliness.

The officer's quarters, where the two flyers were billeted, was on a spit of land called Augusta Huk. On the bay side was Arkona Lighthouse. Opposite, high on the side of Signal Hill near Christ Church, was the impressive Governor's palace of Captain Alfred von Meyer-Waldeck, the German Navy's Commander-in-Chief of the Kiaochow territory. He was a naval officer answering only to the German Minister for the Navy.

Alfred Meyer-Waldeck was born on November 27, 1864 the tenth child of the Professor of German Studies at the University of St. Petersburg. Clemens Friedrich Meyer von Waldeck's title of nobility came from Tsar Alexander II and was passed down to his son Alfred. In 1898, (the year the Germans acquired Tsingtau,) Alfred von Meyer-Waldeck married Johanna Ney, the daughter of a Prussian officer. They had two daughters and a son.

The young Alfred joined the navy and served both afloat and ashore until 1908, when he was sent to Tsingtau about the time that Plüschow was there. He served as Chief-of-Staff from then until 1911, when he became Governor. His tall stature, grey streaked goatee and gentle blue eyes gave him the appearance of a Russian Admiral. He was a tough, and according to his men, a fair taskmaster. Plüschow had the occasion of meeting him briefly when he was a young officer on the *Bismarck* although the Captain wouldn't have remembered him.

Now as a Flying Officer with a celebrated background, he was more than just an average Navy Lieutenant. After reporting in, the two aviators were directed to pay their respects to the Chief-of-Staff and the Governor who were obviously curious to meet the fledgling flyers especially Plüschow, "the world's altitude record holder". The only two things Plüschow and the Governor had in common were their piercing blue eyes and the noble background which the flyer kept to himself although it was rumored. While Meyer-Waldeck with a goatee and moustache was six foot five with a barrel chest and heavy frame, Plüschow was slight but muscular and just under five foot six and clean shaven. But his demeanor, self- assuredness and military bearing made him seem much taller and impressive.

The usual method of transportation for officers and sailors who could afford it were the coolie-drawn rickshaws because walking stained the uniform with sweat in the summer heat. Plüschow would soon rectify this primitive method of travel by obtaining a horse and later an auto from the General Staff.

The flyers learned that the two Rumpler Taube aircraft were still enroute by steamer and not expected before July. Next they visited Iltis Platz which was to be their airport. It was hardly that, merely a flat grassy field used for a race course, parade ground and playing field for various sports. A macadam road, Iltis Platz strasse, ran across the northern one third of the field and a dry stream bed cut across the center. Only 200 meters by 65 meters could actually be used as a landing strip by the aircraft. The field was surrounded by hills over two hundred meters high on all three sides that contained three ferro-concrete fortifications and gun emplacements. The only clear flight path opened was to the southwest and the bay entrance into which jutted the formidable fortress of Hweichuen Point. In Germany this field would have been adequate only for emergency landings, but it was the only flat space available within the protective confines of the city.

Plüschow's Diary:

"The place looked festive and all of Tsingtau was assembled here. In the center of the broad grassy space, a large circle of spectators had gathered around the soccer field. Today was a holiday and an important match between the German sailors and their visiting English seafaring comrades. It was a brilliant game ending 1:1. Today nobody anticipated the events to come."

However Plüschow failed to mention the following:

Admiral Graf von Spee, commander of the German Pacific Fleet, had a splendid silver cup for the winner. With all of the other sporting events averaged, the visiting British sailors won 4 to 3 and were awarded the trophy.

The next day the British put on an elaborate grand ball aboard the *HMS Minotaur*. For the German men and women it was most impressive. An enormous striped tent, held up by a boom, covered 80 feet of the deck amidships between the last of the four smoke stacks and the after deck house. The ten 7.5 inch guns and the four 9.2 inch both fore and aft were festooned with Japanese lanterns. Wood carvings and native war implements from the South Pacific and New Zealand decorated the deck. Dance music was furnished by the ship's band, and specially requisitioned food and drinks were prepared by the officer's galley.

The German women contrasted greatly to the English resident wives or those who were vacationing in Tsingtau. The hair styles remained early 20th Century German with braids coiled up on their heads like large blonde breakfast buns while the coiffeurs of the English ladies were more modern and stylish. There was also dissimilarity in body sizes. The British danced the new tango and foxtrot just becoming popular while the more provincial Germans would only dance German waltzes and polkas that the ship's band considerately played for them.

After the event, a story was circulated and whether true or not struck a sour note with the Germans. It seems that one of the senior British officers, somewhat inebriated, was heard to say, concerning how he liked Tsingtau, "Very nice place indeed!" And under his breath, "Two years more, we have it!"

Some Germans in the General Staff had suspicions that the reason the British paid that particular courtesy call was to reconnoiter the area. For several days and on June 14th in particular Admiral Jerram and his senior officers made a day-long unescorted automobile trip into the countryside along the coast to Lao Shan Harbor. The other officers and sailors had the opportunity to visit the city and take hikes into the hills. It seemed like the entire ship had shore leave. The great number of Britishers spreading like ants over the countryside, disturbed the Germans who could not keep track of so many men.

After the spectacular ball, Admiral Jerram departed with artillery saluting full honors. The signal flags from both German and British squadron commanders spelled out "Live well and goodbye...until we meet again."

Shortly after the British sailed, von Spee stepped up his own preparation and departed. His mission, besides training and honing his men, was to display the Imperial flag to all the German islands across the Pacific.

Meanwhile, Plüschow chose not to remain in the officers' quarters. He located a little villa that was vacant and immediately rented it. It was situated just to the north of the air field nestled amongst trees and other houses where affluent colonials lived. The villa had a front veranda with a good view of the race course and the sea; four nice size rooms including a modern bathroom and kitchen; adjacent servant quarters; chicken coops; a carriage house; a horse stable and a motorcar garage.

Plüschow;

"My life was pure happiness. I had a wonderful command, THE land command of the Navy; a flyer assigned to the cavalry. I had three wonderful years of duty ahead of me. I was in Tsingtau, the paradise on earth and I had my own charming villa high on a hill, with a beautiful view of my airfield and the blue sea. I also had the necessary servants. In order to gain the respect of the Chinese, every European had to surround himself with Chinese servants; it was almost a moral duty."

It also gave employment to the Chinese and helped carry out Meyer-Waldeck's orders that all Germans must learn the native language. Plüschow had six Chinese servants. Moritz the cook who dressed in an elegant blue E-shang, "Mr." Dorsch and "Mr." Simon the house "boys" in charge; Max the lazy gardener; young August the precocious coolie boy who did laundry and ran errands and Fritz the "Mafu" (groom) who smiled constantly and tended the chickens and ducks and shortly after, the horse named Fips which Plüschow acquired. Actually it was a sturdy Mongolian pony which was like those ridden by the German cavalry unit who the Chinese called the "Mountain Navy Horsemen."

To pass the time off duty while awaiting the aircraft, Plüschow would race his "Mongolian" against the cavalrymen around the race course, played polo and would ride with the foreign ladies visiting the summer resort. Despite all this, Plüschow wrote letters home that life in the Far East was rather monotonous for the Europeans.

Plüschow's letter;

"There is no theater, no music, little social life, none of all those things which one hates to miss. The only consolation is that one lives slightly better than under equal circumstances at home."

This letter seemed to be quite the opposite as to what he wrote in his diary. Whether this was to refute his preferential military assignment to a cushy informal post can only be surmised. It was presumed by his fellow officers that Plüschow came from a well-to-do influential background to afford special amenities. They were correct.

Not far from his villa was a large popular vacation resort, the Strand (Beach) Hotel. It was four stories high, situated only fifty meters from the shore and was barely out of the way of his flight path. Along the beach were scores of dressing cabanas and two band stands beneath onion shaped roofs. Every evening in front of the hotel under the trees, the III Seebatlion Marine band would play to an audience of German colonials and International vacationers. They would watch the bathers demurely covered in their full swim costumes, be refreshed by the sea breezes and partake of a variety of alcoholic beverages and coffee or tea. One could always distinguish the nationality of each of the imbibers. While the British would have their whisky sodas, Singapore slings and gin-tonics, Russians would down straight vodka; Frenchmen would sip wine or cognac; Americans would drink anything; Germans would partake of schnapps, brandy or the excellent local German beer from the Germania brewery. The pure spring water for this, even today, world famous "Tsingtao Beer" comes from the mountains of Lao Shan.

Usually they would be joined by Plüschow who would ride up on his "Mongolian" dressed in his conspicuous flying Lieutenant's uniform and decorations and polished riding boots. It was stated by those who knew that "Plüschow was a heroic figure with nerves of steel, extremely self confident with professional experience and he had a zest and joy in living. His upbeat energy, decisiveness and optisism won him the admiration and respect of everyone, especially the women, either married, single or the cabaret "ladies of the evening."

Although Plüschow doesn't exactly say, it could have been

here at the Strand Hotel (SEE PHOTO) that he met an English girl who was vacationing with her parents from Shanghai. He wrote that they saw a lot of each other; rode horses together through the hills, swam, dined and danced. The reader can only surmise what else a single, handsome, navy flyer might do, especially when he had his own private villa.

Plüschow:
"July arrived in all it's beauty. It is the most beautiful month in Tsingtau. Everybody goes to the beach; there were many very nice foreigners, foremost ladies, from the European and American settlements in China and Japan who came to enjoy Tsingtau's beauty and beach life of the "Ostende of the Far East." It was lots of fun. We had horse riding, motoring, polo, and tennis which filled the off-duty hours. Particularly enjoyable were the special gatherings in the evenings when Terpsichore [Greek muse of dancing] was in full demonstration. As in previous years, the English ladies were best represented and soon, charming relationships developed."

Some of the female visitors of various nationalities were actually "ladies of the evening." They were from their winter "houses" in the seaports of Shanghai, Tientsin, HongKong, and Macao and would vacation in Tsingtau during the summer, earning their living and passage money in rented villas that sometimes held up to a dozen girls. The German authorities closed their eyes to such activity.

In response to the news from Europe, on July 7, Admiral Count von Spee ordered the Commanding officer Karl von Muller of the Emden to remain in port pending orders from Germany. The ship was to have sailed for Shanghai the following day. At the same time the Admiral asked von Muller for a complete review of all German naval units in Asia, their exact locations and their state of readiness.

These orders increased the concern of the more wary of the Tsingtau High Command, but the officers made no change in regular exercises, drills, leaves or activities.

As irony would have it, in the middle of July, when the steamer carrying the two Rumpler-Taubes arrived, Linnekogel again broke the world's altitude record by flying to 6560 meters (21,552 feet)!

Both Taubes had been disassembled, each mounted on a specially built four wheel wagon with the wings and tail sections secured on each side of the fuselage, then crated in huge boxes and shipped as deck cargo. The two flyers were on hand when they were unloaded onto the dock. Since there would be no easy way to lift the crates from motor lorries when they reached Iltis Platz, it was decided to remove the birds from the boxes and have them drawn by horse power. The two crates of spare parts were loaded onto a pony cart.

It was quite a sight. The two Tauben were each pulled by two Mongolian ponies guided by a "Ma-fu" (horse handler). Several armed military police walked beside each vehicle while Plüschow and Muellerkowski headed the procession on their Mongolians. This was the first time any Chinese and most of the Europeans had ever seen an aeroplane, albeit looking like giant birds with clipped wings. It seemed like a substantial part of the populace had turned out to watch the flying machines parade through the streets.

A hanger had been constructed at the northern end of the race course to house the aircraft and the two captive balloons and equipment. Plüschow was assigned a crew of petty officers, sailors, mechanics and Chinese coolie workmen to help assemble the structures and machines.

The main fuselage, wheels and engine of the aircraft were already assembled. The latter was a 6 cylinder in-line 100 h.p. water-cooled Daimler-Mercedes engine. (SEE DATA AND PHOTOS) Radiators were against the cowling on each side. The six engine exhausts were piped downward to the rear on the right side.

Top speed was rated at 75 m.p.h. (although this was debatable)

24

and fuel for four hours at cruising speed gave it a range of 250 miles. The ceiling for this particular model was 3,500 meters (11,500 feet).

The frame was of steel tubing welded and bolted together and covered with "balloon cloth" a linen-like material sealed on the outside with a rubberized "dope." The seats in this model were made of light weight wood and the nose cowling was aluminum.

The 21 foot wings were first to be attached to the body. They looked very much like a bird's wing, the bones being the double wood framing held apart by wood spacers. But to make the wings flexible and controllable by the aileron warp method, bamboo slats were secured at the trailing edge of each wing. The scallop effect, so similar to the feathered wing of a bird, was because of the material being stretched so tightly. There was a space of 15 centimeters between the fuselage and the wings.

Just between the two cockpits, minus wind screens, a vertical inverted "V" strut or king-post was secured through which eight steel piano wires, 2 and 3 mm diameters, were attached to strategic parts of the wings. At the outer edge of each wing was a vertical strut or stanchion through which six wires fanned out to the trailing edge of the wing frames both on top and underneath. This enabled the ailerons to be warped both up or down very similar to a bird's wing in flight. Then the control wires were led back through pulley fairleads to the cockpit controls on both sides by way of various leads and the king-post between the two cockpits.

A wooden automobile-type steering wheel was used for wing warping and attached to a stick for elevator action. (SEE THE COCKPIT PHOTO). A pivoting rudder bar, operated with the feet, controlled the vertical surfaces of the split rudders one each above and below the fan tail. Instruments included an altimeter, fuel gage, water-temperature gage and a tachometer. In some models a compass, clock and inclinometer were sometimes installed. Plüschow would carry a pocket watch and a hand compass.

On the underside of the wings was a ladder shaped brace of

steel tubing that ran from the body to the outer lower vertical brace. This with guy wires fanning out fore and aft to the wing gave it rigidity. The wires were tightened with small locking brass turnbuckles.

The tail was what really gave the Taube the look of a dove. It fanned out horizontally from just behind the rear cockpit and was likewise supported and controlled by a vertical king-post and guy wires. The vertical rudder was hinged, one section above and one below the horizontal tail. The rudders were both controlled together with 4 mm wire that led into the rear cockpit through both sides of the fusalage. A large metal drag skid held the tail off the ground. The myriad of guy wires gave it the look of a ship's rigging and the sound of the "wind in the wires" was a fairly good technique of estimating air speed. This was truly a ship that flew like a bird!

The landing gear was fitted with two oversize bicycle wheels and would pivot through spring shocks that only slightly absorbed the impact of landing. For fledgling pilots and inexperienced sailors, the instructions to assemble the Taubes must have been complicated to say the least. Plüschow had only flown the planes, not assembled them, although he had carefully studied every aspect of their features when awaiting his flying lessons. That knowledge, together with his record breaking altitude flight, made him the senior ranking pilot. The official designation of the plane assigned to Plüschow was Rumpler, Navy No. E-8. The other plane was Rumpler, Navy No. E-1 both delivered to the German navy late in 1913. The E-8 was several months newer. Both were the predecessors of the Rumpler-Taube 4C that broke the altitude record, but never-the-less they were the type that Plüschow had learned to fly.

The Taube monoplane evolved from the observation of Dr. Fredrich Ahlborn, a German naturalist. He discovered that the dried Zanonia seed from Java (now called Indonesia) glided in a stable fashion like a tiny "flying wing." In 1898 Dr. Ahlborn wrote that; "A flying-machine of similar shape would inherit these desirable aerodynamic properties."

Experiments with Zanonia shaped gliders during the first few years of the 20th Century eventually evolved to powered flight.

When a bird-like tail and body was added to the aircraft, giving it the look of a Leonardo da Vinci sketch, it came to be known as the "Dove," or "Pigeon," TAUBE in German.

The monoplane soon proved its popularity in Europe. Between 1910 and the end of 1914, when their heyday ended, fifty-four aircraft companies, mostly in Austria and Germany, manufactured some 500 varieties of the Tauben (pl). A few of the builders were Etrich, Halberstadt, Dannegger, Ehrlich, Lohner, Euler, Fokker, Gallone, Goedecker, Gotha, Hansa, Harlan, Jatho, Jeannin, Klein, Kondor, Rumpler, Sohlmann, Schulze, Steffen Westphal and Zeigler. The Taube designation was always prefaced by the builder's name. Etrich, the Austrian and Rumpler in Germany were the two most notable of the aircraft engineers and builders.

As the weather was hot and dry, the plane was assembled at the door of the hanger in full view. The spectators, both Chinese and foreigners alike sat on the hillsides and on the race course, but kept at a distance by police. They watched in awe as the first Fei-ji "Fly-machine" took shape. Many believed it would be assembled in a few hours and then take off and fly. They had to wait longer than that.

Plüschow:
"We hardly had any rest. Day and night we worked to assemble the aircraft, and two days later, very early, my plane was ready to fly."

(Author's note: probably when Plüschow entered his diary, but it was actually the 3rd day; July 28 1914)

"When the sun began to rise, the propeller turned and the engine started. I pushed hard on the accelerator, rolled across the field and lifted into the air. The airfield began to look very small. But on this wonderful sunny morning, I did not worry and happily flew wide circles over Tsingtau, waking up hundreds of surprised people with the noise of the motor. When I prepared for the landing, I was a bit nervous. How small the landing space really was! I flew more circles and postponed the critical moment of landing. But I couldn't stay in the air forever."

By the time Plüschow had gathered enough courage to land, a crowd of onlookers had thronged to the race-course by the Strand Hotel. Chinese and foreigners, tourists or military men, none except the other pilot had ever seen an aircraft in powered flight. The area had to be cordoned off and made a restricted zone, else the crowds would have obstructed the field trying to get closer to this flying marvel. The plane made several passes over the field getting a little lower each time. The deep throated growl of the engine accelerated as the plane swept gracefully into the air. The warp controls moving the trailing edge of wings and tail made it look alive like a giant bird in flight. Luckily the light breeze was from the north west and he had an easy approach into it from the bay.

This was the first International Schau'flug, "air show" in China with spectators from Germany, England, France, Russia, United States, Canada, China and Japan. Takahashi the local photographer was on hand to document the event as were several reporters including A.M. Brace the American Associated Press correspondent. Women with colorful parasols sat on the porch of the resort hotel for a better view, and men folk who knew next to nothing of the subject, discussed the pros and cons of the "aeroplane." The festive throngs were not relegated as usual to the best vantage point by rank or skin color. It seemed that Tsingtau had taken an International holiday.

Plüschow's trepidation was soon alleviated when he saw the waving crowds and he brought the Fei-ji, "Fly-machine," as the

Chinese called it, to a near perfect landing. The crowds cheered and broke through the police lines to swarm about the plane and the smiling pilot. Even though the Taube looked like it was designed from a Leonardo da Vinci sketch this fledgling "Dove" could fly, and to great heights. When the Chinese dragon tattoo on the flyer's bare left arm was observed, the populace immediately gave Lieutenant Gunther Plüschow the title of "Lung Gong-tau"...."Dragon Master."

By coincidence Baron Yasimasa Fukuschima, the Japanese Governor of Kwantung, which Japan had captured from Russia in 1905, was in Tsingtau on a long term study of the German civil administration. The Baron had served as an attache in Berlin from 1887 to 1892 and knew the German language and customs.

When he left Germany, Fukuschima traveled home by horse-back across Russia, a trip lasting over a year which earned him the admiration of the Germans. The Baron learned Russian and certainly much valuable military information that was instrumental in Japan's successful attack against Port Arthur in 1904-05 and subsequently conquering the entire Kwantung province.

The Baron had observed the Taube's first flight from atop the Governor's palace and was most impressed that the Germans had introduced aircraft into their colony's defenses. Meyer-Waldeck minimized any strategic usefulness of the "flying kite."

On July 30, Tsingtau received reports of the outbreak of hostilities between Serbia and Austria-Hungary. Meyer-Waldeck refused suggestions for any mobilization which might embarrass his pleasant guest. The Baron decided suddenly to depart Tsingtau pending the resolution of the European hostilities. A festive farewell dinner was provided by the officers of the garrison. They exchanged friendly speeches and goodbyes and toasted Plüschow's successful flight and air-show.

Plüschow's first flight was written up in the Shanghai, Tientsin and Peking newspapers in several languages. Thinking to downplay the military applications, the German authorities tried to describe the aircraft, as "merely a toy". This was exactly the opinion of their superiors in the Imperial German High Command at that period. Pilots were merely thought of as flying chauffeurs. It was customary that officers were the observers, while only petty officers and non-coms piloted the plane. Plüschow was one of the exceptions; he wanted to be able to do both. Hence technically as an observer-pilot he was assigned to the cavalry who also performed reconnaissance missions.

No matter what the Tsingtau general staff thought, the navy-flyer was now even more popular in the social circles. But Plüschow had little time for play as he was in charge of assembling Muellerkowski's plane.

Plüschow:

"A polo competition was planned with the English Polo Club of Shanghai for the beginning of August. But, on July 30, suddenly the order to "secure" Tsingtau reached us. I remember it as if it were today. Very early, an orderly came to our villa and gave Patiz (his petty officer aid-de-camp) and myself the order to report immediately to the Division Commander. Of course, we thought that this was only an exercise. I grumbled about the interruption of our sleep, as we had worked late, but never-the- less left immediately to report. Here we received confirmation of the hardly believable message. Still firmly doubting that there would be a war, we hurried to our battle stations, the airfield, and began with the necessary preparations. The message "Threat of War," which reached us the next day brought us confirmation."

It was July 31st. Baron Fukuschima and his entourage had just left by train. Marine Lieutenant Muellerskowski insisted on flying his Taube which had just been assembled. It was late afternoon. The sea breeze had freshened. Plüschow tried to have him postpone the flight until the next day but to no avail; the Marine flyer was not under his authority.

Muellerskowski's objective was more than just a test flight. He wanted to undertake a reconnaissance and orientation mission up the coast for possible deployment sites for the III Seebatalion and take some of the glory away from his counterpart.

Plüschow did share his previous experience of taking off and landing on the tiny field and warned him of the changing air currents. He tried again to have him delay his flight but the Marine flyer took off anyway. When he was airborne, having flown for only a few minutes and just clearing some trees at the end of the field, a gust of on-shore wind updrafted from the low embankment by the beach and Muellerskowski seemingly panicked. The plane nosed up sharply, stalled and crashed sideways to the ground from a height of over 50 meters. (165 ft.) The Taube was a total wreck and the Marine Lieutenant was hospitalized with multiple fractures. He was the first German casualty of the impending campaign. The local Japanese postcard photographer on hand was forbidden by the Germans to take pictures.

There was one reported rumor that the crash of Muellerkowski was somehow partly due to the jealously between the two flyers, the inference being left to the reader. But this could hardly have been the case since witnesses heard Plüschow try vehemently to persuade the Marine to delay his flight. Muellerkowski possibly wanted to be on record as the first to fly an assigned reconnaissance mission for Germany in China. Technically he was.

And so it was that the day before Germany declared war against Russia on August 1, 1914, and two days before invading Luxembourg, just prior to declaring war on France and England, Germany lost half of its fledgling air force in Tsingtau.

# CHAPTER 3

## WAR IN EUROPE
## TSINGTAU MOBILIZES
## BALLOON FLIGHT
## JAPANESE ULTIMATUM

The disastrous crash of Muellerkowski only vindicated the low regard the senior and even the junior officers had toward the flimsy aircraft and the surviving playboy pilot. Plüschow had to overcome a lot of jealously and resentment against him, as well as prove the military usefulness of his aircraft.

There is an old German axiom that army officers look wiser than they are, and naval officers are wiser than they look. Plüschow, being a naval officer added an additional dimension to the axiom. He, as an aviator, would look the part by dressing impeccably. But he would also be even wiser by studying the theories and ideas of the early aeronautical pioneers. At every opportunity he expounded his knowledge to his fellow officers.

Plüschow had studied the "Rules for the use of Aeroplanes in War", written in 1911 by Giulio Douhet, the commander of Italy's Aeronautical Battalion which consisted mainly of reconnaissance balloons. Douhet sneered at those who said that bombing of cities was barbaric, and reminded his readers that in every European country most of the factories producing guns, ammunition and other weapons of war were located in the midst of cities. If a nation's aerial forces can create intolerable conditions within the enemies territory, like fear, hunger, panic, loss of production and immobility, they must capitulate no matter what the status of it's ground forces. Destroy the head of the octopus and the arms will wither and die.

Douhet's theories were not military secrets; they were published in Italian newspapers and aeronautical magazines and of course his "Rules for the use of Aeroplanes in War" was not classified. It was surprising that no major power took his ideas seriously except one, the Japanese. In 1912 their fledgling Army and Naval air forces were instructed by the French using Maurice Farman bi-wing pusher land and hydroplanes.

There was one Frenchman who also had the vision to foresee the future of aircraft as a weapon, but hardly anyone paid much attention to him either. He was Captain Ferdinand Ferber, one of the earliest disciples of Bleriot, Santos-Dumont, the Wright brothers and the Italian Douhet. In 1911 he was interviewed by a French aviation magazine. The reporter, after hearing his theories of the aeroplane's potential in warfare, asked in honest surprise,

"But how could a battle actually take place between two aeroplanes?"

The visionary aeronautical pioneer said prophetically, "In the same method as birds fight. When a hawk, for instance, wants to attack a pigeon, it first pursues it; and as soon as the pigeon finds itself overtaken, it ascends in spirals, and the hawk starts to rise in a parallel line. If the pigeon can fly higher than the hawk it is free; if it cannot, its only recourse is to plummet to earth, although during the descent it is liable to be intercepted by the hawk. Every time the hawk darts upon the pigeon, the latter will try, by means of a clever sideslip, to avoid capture. If the hawk has been eluded, there is respite, for carried beyond its target, the hawk loses altitude which it must regain. The race for altitude may begin once more, but then if the hawk gains superiority, the pigeon will finally alight on the ground and unless it can get under shelter, it will be caught. In a like manner, will aerial craft struggle."

The magazine did not dismiss Captain Ferber's ideas as absurdities, but commented, "Until exceptionally large and fast aeroplanes are built, and able to throw explosives by guns or bombs, these theories must remain more or less theoretical." The magazine also added, "Great nations should beware of the grim potentialities Captain Ferber warns us against."

The early Japanese aviators learning to fly by the French took note of these revolutionary theories. So did the German pilot Plüschow. Soon they would confront each other.

Plüschow;

"Even though a German colony and naval base, Tsingtau was International. Here there were Russian, French, Japanese and English living or visiting as guests among us. There was a clash of opinions and emotions which could not have happened in any other part of the world. The most important question, I repeat, THE question which occupied us all: Will there be a war with England?

On the second of August, we made our offer to England. I was riding with my English lady friend and of course, this topic became the main subject of conversation. In the opinion of my companion, which corresponded with the one that all her friends and acquaintances had, was that a war between England and Germany was unthinkable. Otherwise the prestige of the white race would be lost in the Far East and the yellow Japs (direct quote) would laughingly harvest the fruits of our conflict. The same thought also preoccupied us Germans; in particular among us Naval Officers nothing else was discussed."

At noon on the first of August people gathered at the bulletin outside the Government Haus and at the bank on Kaiser Wilhelm strasse and saw the red official notices which read; "The Kaiser has ordered the mobilization of all army and marine reserves." The Governor had received a telegram to announce the alert and to prepare for the imminent possibility of war with England, France and Russia.

Plüschow;

Only three days after Muellerskowski had his accident, I started my first extended survey flight. The weather was beautiful. After flying over the entire area hundreds of kilometers beyond Tsingtau, I returned. I was at an altitude of 1,500 meters and landing was particularly difficult because of aerial conditions. I had to land into the wind which was from the north and the mountains encircling the tiny field caused turbulence. I then had engine trouble. When accelerating, the engine choked, sputtered and died. Instead of being able to circle once, I had to make an emergency landing. On the right side was the polo club and on the left the Strand Hotel. I couldn't turn left or right. My only thought was to keep the Mercedes engine safe. There were no engine spare parts. I hoped to land on a small wooded area on top of the trees, but the plane had dropped too low. I pulled the altitude-steering back as hard as I could. I could just see over the wires. Then I pulled my knees up. The plane landed heavily, rolled a short distance and the wheels hit a ditch at the edge of the racecourse and the plane nosed over, but not completely. It was left standing nearly upright in the ditch. Part of the body and a wing was a mass of bent steel tubes, wood splinters wires and cloth. The propeller was broken. The engine was safe. I was not injured."

Five spare propellers and various support structures for the Taubes had been shipped from Germany, but when Plüschow opened the crates he finds disaster. The cases had apparently been stored on the deck of the ship and rain, sea and tropical dampness had made them unusable. The coils of spare wires and fabric were badly rusted, mildewed and decayed. All the laminated propellers had split apart and warped. If the tip deviates only 4 to 5 mm from true it would cause concern, but these propellers were warped up to 20 centimeters (nearly 8 inches)! The senior marine engineer of the dock area Mr. Stuben, two Germans of the engine department Frinks and Scholl and eight Chinese from the dock crew, set to work to reconstruct and repair the damage to body and wings.

Then the least damaged propeller was given to the model maker to form a template. This Chinese expert was more than just a model maker and carpenter, he was an experienced cabinet maker of fine furniture. Under his supervision seven weathered strips of oak were glued together with the best furniture adhesive they had. Then with axes, adzes, planes and abrasives, the wood was shaped to fit the template model. All the work was painstakingly done by hand like it has been for centuries in China.

On August 4, in the evening the news arrived: The war against England had been declared! Next morning R.H. Eckford the British vice-consul visited Meyer-Waldeck who was his close friend and golfing partner and showed him a succinct dispatch from London, "War, ask passport." Eckford and Meyer-Waldeck expressed their sincere regrets over the conflict and wished each other the best of fortunes until they met again.

Now the next question; what would Japan do as England's ally? As the threat of hostilities increased, the tourists emptied the hotels and resort villas and departed Tsingtau by rail and ship. The French, Russians and British residents fled, selling as much of their property as was possible. But the two hundred fifty Japanese stayed on and watched with astute interest. They did not sell their properties, but neither did they buy any of the other discounted holdings that were for sale.

There was a photographer's shop owned by T. Takahashi. The Japanese was renowned for his humor, and knowledge of German and Western cultural ethics and customs. His good will and toothy smiling friendliness was irresistible. His photographs were of the highest state-of-the-art and his quality picture postcards of the area made superb souvenirs. Even the German Naval Captain, Meyer-Waldeck had commissioned Takahashi to take the official pictures when he became Governor of Tsingtau in 1911. Meyer-Waldeck's imposing height of 1.95 meters (6 foot 5 inches) was in sharp contrast to the very short photographer. Takahashi was an institution, with considerable freedom of movement, up until now. But unbeknownst to the Germans at that time, he was also a Japanese spy.

Takahashi had been intently interested in the two aircraft and was always on hand to take pictures of the ascents and landings. But when the Germans prohibited Muellerkowski's humiliating crash to be photographed by the Japanese he surreptitiously took the photos anyway, likewise when Plüschow had his accident. (SEE PHOTO)

German counter-intelligence had led the Japanese to believe that the strength of the Tsingtau garrison was a little over one thousand men. That was how many rotational replacements arrived aboard the steamship Patricia on June 2. Actually the total garrison was 3098. Takahashi had been allowed to take pictures of the ships leaving and arriving but he always framed the scene to include the German warships and military installations in the background. Several of his photos have been discovered in historical archives.

During the first few weeks of August, German reservists from all over Asia converged on Tsingtau for mobilization, some as far away as Siam. This was mostly a conglomerate group — members of paramilitary organizations in China, various gun clubs and aging and paunchy civilians.

There was even a German sergeant in the French Foreign Legion stationed in Indo-China who deserted. He was nearly caught by French officers in a hotel near the Chinese border. Wearing civilian clothes, he jumped to attention when the two Legionnaire Lieutenants entered the bar. Pretending not to speak French, he said in German that he was Swiss. They didn't believe him but were in no position to arrest the deserter as the ex-sergeant was over six foot six. Unlikely as it seems, he travelled with a Chinese friend to Tsingtau through China by train disguised as a Chinese coolie by dying his blonde hair black, shaving his beard and eyebrows and pretending to be speechless.

There were Embassy and Consulate guards from Peking and Tientsin; German sailors on British merchant vessels who jumped ship; business men from every city in China and Japan where Germans worked; and the German unit from the Shanghai Volunteer Corps, an International civilian militia. They arrived with their weapons hidden in their steamer trunks having paid much "cumshaw" to the Shanghai Customs.

The largest contingent were the East Asian Marine Detachment consisting of 450 men who were stationed at Tienstin some 300 miles north of Tsingtau. Some of the men had made their way to Tsingtau before war was declared. But now they faced the possibility of being interned by the neutral Chinese. Under the very able Lieutenant Colonel Paul Kuhlo the men pretended to march out of the city on maneuvers in groups of 20 and 30. The Chinese knew they couldn't march all the way to Tsingtau, but what they didn't know was that arrangements had been made for a train to be waiting for them outside the city.

The Germans with the help of the guards at the Austrian embassy were also able to dismantle and smuggle their weapons in crates marked as machinery and building material aboard another train bound for Tsingtau. They included a number of machine guns and three 150mm howitzers and three 80mm field pieces Several Irishmen who worked the railroad and who hated the British helped to smuggle the men and weapons past the British, Japanese and French who tried to put pressure on the Chinese to prevent the Germans from getting to Tsingtau. When the men finally got through after picking up a handful more reservists at Tsinanfu, they were all met with jubilation upon arriving at the Tapautau station.

A most unique historical event was documented by Kurt Meissner, an eye witness, and written by Jefferson Jones in the book

"The Fall of Tsingtau, with a Study of Japan's Ambitions in China." published by Houghton Mifflin Co. in 1915.

"In Japan the departees of various nations received their most memorable send-off. The scenes of departing soldiers (reservists) provided many vignettes for history. There were crowds of French, British, Austrians and Germans leaving for the war; in many instances they departed on the same ships. The Japanese supported the Germans with an unexpected warmth. By the hundreds they crowded Yokohama and Kobe, shouting "banzai" and "sayonnara" to the Germans. They gave the departees presents of food and drink which sustained them for many weeks. The Germans reported these experiences when arriving in Tsingtau as clear indications of popular Japanese support for their cause."

There were three times as many reservists arriving as Meyer-Waldeck estimated through consular reports. The reserves would finally number 76 officers and 1400 men.

Depending on their expertise, many employees proved senior in military rank to their bosses. Because of the hasty induction and the unexpected numbers, the quartermaster people soon ran out of uniforms. The result was that improvised uniforms of strange colors gave the reservists the look of rag-tag revolutionaries.

These irregular, nonprofessional looking men worried the regular soldiers as to the reservists' proficiency. Regardless, the esprit-de-corps and the single mindedness of purpose was contagious. The Governor, with the rank of Navy Captain, headed the military bureaucracy along with his role as the commander of the fortress now totaling 4574 men. However, only four thousand were capable of fighting.

Tsingtau's population, exclusive of the garrison, was about 65,000 of whom some 2600 were Europeans, most of whom had left. The greatest hysteria to the impending war came from the Chinese.

They fled the city in large numbers. Those who could not leave by the railroad went on foot or horse cart. Others sought passage on the hundreds of sampans and fishing junks that took them across Kaiochow Bay to the fishing village of Taputau in Chinese territory. These refugees, especially the men, were a crucial part of the city's work force, and their departure threatened the labor pool. Someone in the general staff suggested building concentration camps to prevent the exodus of the native workers. Meyer-Waldeck wisely rejected the idea. Instead he increased the pay for all laborers. That, together with the lack of actual hostilities, brought the Chinese coolies back to work. They were paid in cash and coin each working day.

Plüschow's servants, who lived in quarters behind his villa, were also concerned, but a slight increase in pay helped to alleviate their fears. Actually they had no place to go. Their ancestral homes in the country were still within German territory and as yet there was no indication of hostilities.

With the exodus of most of the servants working in German households, the women, used to comfortable colonial living, now had to do the menial coolie work they were unaccustomed to.

All the able-bodied German men of Tsingtau were asked to form a militia defense force. Others were enlisted to supplement the German and Chinese policemen who would control possible unrest of the Chinese populace.

Meyer-Waldeck appealed to the women of Tsingtau to volunteer as nurses. They came from every social status; from the wives of wealthy business men and officials to wives of ordinary sailors and marines; From banker's wives to bar maids they volunteered in great numbers. Only 85 were chosen and the doctors and nurses began instructing them in nursing duties. Other women set to work to cut and fold bandages. The Hotel Prince Heinrich ballroom was carefully cleaned with carbolic acid solution so that it could be used as another hospital. Scores of cots were put in place.

Four ladies took charge over the kitchen duties and food

"acquisition" (it was called shopping) with the help of a few dedicated Chinese women who remained. Up every day at 5 o'clock, they cooked three meals a day for over 200 people. They also made a nursery for the children so the wives could be free to help where needed.

On August 7, Meyer-Waldeck received a report that the Japanese were in Harbin discussing strategy with the Russians. The Japanese had fought against them in 1904-05 and won. Both nations were now allies. The two countries were talking about spheres of influence in China, including a Japanese siege and occupation of Tsingtau. Other events also altered the optimistic German outlook that war in the Far East might be averted.

The small Japanese colony, about 250 persons, suddenly began closing and boarding up their businesses and homes and started leaving. This was especially significant now that their movements were restricted, especially Takahashi's photography. The Japanese press throughout Asia ceased its pro-German position and began a nasty anti-German official profile. No longer was there much doubt of Japan's intention regarding Tsingtau.

While waiting for the new propeller to be built and carefully balanced, Plüschow had another task to accomplish.

Plüschow's diary:

"I had another job to do because I was in charge of the captive balloons, the fat competition to my Dove. In Germany I had taken a course in balloon aviation which consisted of free balloon navigation and practice handling of a captive balloon, including how to fill it with gas, as well as repair work.

In Tsingtau we had two big balloons, 2000 cubic meters each and all the necessary equipment to produce gas to fill them. Iltis Platz was the location for the installation, but out of the way of the landing pattern for my Taube. A Navy petty officer who also had been trained briefly as a balloonist, and myself were the only ones who had any experience.

After stretching out the material we proceeded carefully to fill it. We were proud when the first "Yellow Sausage," as the men called it, lay half inflated. My Petty Officer and I personally tied each control line. Soon the yellow monster rose slowly into the air."

It was a novel sight to the gawking Chinese who had never witnessed a balloon of this size. They had only seen the two meter diameter weather balloons sent up from signal hill. The kite balloon or "Drachen" was a hydrogen-filled torpedo-shaped envelope with tail fins to keep it stabilized into the wind. It was about 200 feet long and 50 feet in diameter. Below this powerless gas bag was suspended an open wicker basket for one or two men. It contained a parachute which was stored in a conical enclosure, large end open and facing downward. In the event of trouble the observer slipped the parachute cords onto a harness that he wore and jumped over the side of the basket, pulling the parachute from its container.

The balloon was attached to a powerful high-speed motorized ground winch by means of a stout cable. Each balloon installation included a hydrogen gas generator, spare balloon, repair parts and ground-to-air telephone equipment.

Plüschow continues:

"Then we brought it back down with the winch. I alone climbed into the basket for the first flight. It almost was my free balloon trip back to the Fatherland. When the start signal was given, the attachment cable was held too loosely and the balloon jumped up about 50 meters into the air and jerked the cable very hard. I had but one thought; it's going to get loose and fly off. There was another bump and I almost fell out of the basket. The cable was new and withstood the strain. Soon with systematic training and practice of my team, all went well as if we had always been experienced balloon aviators.

The government had high hopes for the balloon. They expected it to assist in the observation of any approaching enemy and to locate the enemy's artillery. Unfortunately they were wrong, and my fears with respect to the use of the balloon installation at Iltis Platz, proved to be true.

Although I had brought the balloon up as high as 1200 meters, we were not able to see beyond the hills which circled our position."

This location was determined to be unsatisfactory for the reconnaissance balloons and they were moved to a sweet potato field on the outskirts of Tai Tung-Tschen six kilometers north of the city. The Chinese village was just inside the German defense line that stretched some seven kilometers across the Tsingtau peninsular from the Yellow Sea to Kiaochow Bay. While the distances might seem minuscule, it must be emphasized that transportation at that time was primitive. Even if the roads were good, much of getting about was on foot and over hilly terrain.

On August 15, 1914 a demand from Japan was received by Meyer-Waldeck via submarine telegraph cable which was soon after cut by the British. The Japanese Ambassador in Berlin delivered the identical message to the Kaiser.

The Japanese ultimatum;

*"Under the present conditions we deem it very important and necessary to take measures which will remove the cause of all disturbances of the peace in the Far East and safeguard the common interest, which is the essence of the Japanese-British treaty. In order to safeguard a firm and enduring peace in East Asia, the maintenance of which is the main goal of this treaty, the Imperial Japanese*

*Government believes it to be its sincere duty to advise the Imperial German Government to carry out the two suggestions:*

*1. To recall immediately all German warships and auxiliary cruisers of all types from Japanese and Chinese waters and to disarm all those vessels which cannot be recalled.*

*2. To hand over by September 15, without conditions and without compensation, to the Imperial Japanese authorities, who will, if warranted, return it to China, the leasehold of Kiautschou.*

*The Imperial Japanese Government at the same time advises that if it does not receive the answer of the Imperial German Government, agreeing to the unconditional acceptance of the advice of the Imperial Japanese Government, by noon of August 23, 1914, it will be forced to take steps it deems necessary in view of the situation."*

The Governor issued a proclamation which was posted at several locations about Tsingtau and was read at roll-call;

*"On August 15, Japan issued an ultimatum to Germany, in which was demanded the immediate recall of all German warships and cruiser squadrons, as well as the unconditional surrendering of Tsingtau by September 15. The deadline for reply was noon of August 23, 1914.*

*This unheard-of demand is insulting in tone as well as in content. We will never voluntarily give up even the smallest piece of land on which flies the German flag. We will not yield from this place, where, for the past 17 years we have tried, with devotion and success, to create a small Germany across the sea. If the enemy wants Tsingtau, let him come and get it. He will find us at our positions. Therefore we look to the future with confidence, well prepared to meet the enemy!"*

With concurrence from his senior officers, the Governor sent a concise dispatch to Kaiser Wilhelm II stating his intention.

*"I guarantee the utmost fulfillment of duty."*

There was no doubt as to Meyer-Waldeck's position and resolve. The prompt reply from the naval headquarters in Berlin was equally succinct.

*"His Majesty has ordered the defense of Tsingtau to the bitter end."*

# CHAPTER 4

## DEFENSES STRENGTHENED;
## GERMAN COMMAND CHAIN

Fearing entrapment, the light cruiser *Emden*, had put to sea on July 31, the same day that Muellerkowski crashed his plane. On August 4, a few days after war was declared between Germany and Russia, she captured a 3,500 ton Russian steamer, *Rajasan* in the shipping lane between Nagasaki and Vladivostok. Commander von Muller brought his first prize of the Far Eastern conflict back to Tsingtau and the ship was renamed *Cormoran*. The vessel was outfitted and placed in commission as an auxiliary raider to rendezvous with von Spee's units in the South Pacific. The Russian crew was repatriated to neutral Chinese territory. Shortly after, the new *Cormoran* followed the *Emden* out of port on August 9, the last warship leaving Tsingtau.

The capture of the Russian ship was viewed with much displeasure by the Japanese who considered the German action as an affront to their sovereignty by invading their neutral territorial waters almost at their front door.

Von Spee's fleet had sailed for the South Pacific several weeks previously to join with several other warships in the area. The ships were the armored cruisers *Scharnhorst* and *Gneisenau* and light cruisers *Leipzig, Nurnbers, Dresden*, and the *Emden*. With them were eleven German freighters carrying supplies for the raiding warships. They had loaded 19,000 tons of coal, 120 tons of machine oil and a tremendous amount of food, drinking water and other provisions at

Tsingtau before they departed.

Remaining in port at Meyer-Waldeck's disposal, were four old gunboats; the outdated warship *Jaguar*, an old destroyer torpedo-boat S-90, the minelayer *Lauting* and the antiquated Austrian unarmored cruiser *Kaiserin Elisabeth*. Built in 1890, she displaced 4,000 tons and her six 150 mm (5.9 inch) guns were not a major threat to any armored naval unit. Her allegiance at the time was uncertain. Several German river gunboats operating in China had quietly slipped into Tsingtau, and the guns, ammunition and crew had been removed for use in the land defense.

At the offset if was not known if Austria would be involved in the war. Captain Makoviz received orders from his superiors to neutralize the vessel and evacuate his crew to Tientsin. His government would not be involved in Asia where it had no military force except an old cruiser. He did have secret sealed instructions that succinctly said, "in case of war he was to operate in the best interests of the Three-Power Alliance," namely Germany Austria-Hungary. But on the 24th Captain Makoviz received confirmation orders to deactivate the vessel and evacuate the crew to Tientsin.

Makoviz ordered a watch crew of only eighteen men to stay behind. He also decided to remain aboard ship. That evening he sadly watched 8 staff officers and 391 men leave the city.

Their train trip to Tientsin was very unpleasant for the *Elizabeth's* crew. Europeans and Chinese alike demonstrated through obscene gestures and jeers that the Austrian cowards were running from the war. Less than an hour after they arrived at their destination, they received new orders, confirmed from Vienna that they were to return to their original station in Tsingtau.

This posed serious problems for the Austrian crew now in Tientsin. They had to return before the neutral Chinese would be obliged to intern them. In a few days with forged papers and in civilian clothes gathered from the German and Austrian community, small groups slipped out of the city by train and canal boat. It took several weeks before all the crew of the Elizabeth rejoined the ship.

Austria is the only nation that offered the exclusive decoration for successfully disobeying orders; the Maria Theresa medal. Captain Makoviz now wished with all his heart he had earned that award! The naval infantry battalion and the East Asiatic Naval Detachment contained only land troops, despite the "naval" designation. The reason for employing this unusual organization came from the structure of the German military system of that time. The navy was the Imperial Navy and hence came under the Empire. The German army, however, belonged to the federated states, like today's national guard or militia, and each chain of command controlled its own resources. The confusion of a garrison of army troops would pose complications especially when the Imperial Diet appropriated funds for troops sent abroad. It was more logical to meet this expense with the navy budget. The ranks, uniforms and traditions of the German troops in China were naval. The education and training was army.

The Third Naval Battalion consisted of five companies designated III SeeBatalion (Marines). One was a mounted company, which the Chinese called the "Mountain Navy Horsemen," a field artillery battery, an engineer company, two horse-drawn machine gun brigades, and the Fifth Naval Artillery unit that manned the fortifications. (The breakdown is towards the end of the book.)

The Military Bureau consisted of the General staff, Signal & Wireless Telegraph Station, Naval Bureau, Ordnance Department, Mine Department, The Observatory and Intelligence. Plüschow was assigned to the last category... Intelligence.

In order to fly effective aerial reconnaissance missions, the terrain in and around Tsingtau had to be observed from the ground. It was imperative that Plüschow, locate aerial navigational aids and newly established military installations and fix them on his maps. This was the opportune time as the aircraft's new propeller was still being constructed and the flyer grounded. The Lieutenant and his petty officer acquired a staff car to survey the area. Together with intelligence officers at general headquarters in the Governor's Palace they planned their route. An Oberleutnant intelligence officer of Meyer-Waldeck's general staff also accompanied them.

On the charts, Tsingtau lies 708 kilometers (440 miles) north of Shanghai and 900 kilometers (558 miles) northwest from the Japanese naval bases of Sasebo and Nagasaki.

The city proper lies at the end of a peninsula forming the northern arm enclosing Kiaochow Bay. The Hai-hsi peninsula, with Cape Jaeschke at its tip, forms the southern arm. The entrance between is only 4 kilometers (2.5 miles) wide and has a depth of over 25 meters (100 feet).

The Kiaochow treaty district lies between Kiaochow Bay on the west and Lao Shan (Old Mountain) bay on the east. The Pai-Sha Ho, or White Sand River forms the northern boundary, and the Yellow Sea the southern. The city of Tsingtau lies on the southwest point of the peninsula. SEE MAPS

Tsingtau had never been given adequate military preparations for a major conflict. Some of the shore batteries only had five shells each, which made them next to useless. But these were old 240 mm Chinese cannons situated by the inner harbor.

The most important fortifications had considerably more. The major land batteries were on Bismarck and Iltis Hills. The latter had six 120 mm, two 105 mm guns, four 60 mm cannon and other assorted pieces.

Bismarck Fort lay just to the north of the Iltis Platz flying field and up the mountain behind Plüschow's villa. It was an immense ferro-concrete bastion constructed in three sections buried deep into the hill top. This 135 meter (443 feet) high fortress mounted four 280 mm (11 inch) howitzers and four 155 mm (6 inch) guns. It had an excellent overview to the northern land approaches as well as seaward. The fort was complete with fire-control stations, passageways, narrow gage railroad from the main external ammunition depot, ammunition hoists, cooking and eating facilities, living quarters and everything to make it a state-of-the art military stronghold.

As protection from a sea attack, the Hweichuen Fort was likewise massive and heavily reinforced. It lay on a point of land 1200 meters due south of the airfield. Landing from seaward, Plüschow could use the site as a navigation marker.

Built of solid reinforced concrete several meters thick it was set into the 33 meter high (110 foot) elevation of the rocky headland. The interior length was slightly over 280 meters (over 900 feet). On each side of the numerous passageways were living quarters, toilet facilities, diesel generators for electricity, machine shops, store rooms, ventilation blowers, an immaculate galley, mess rooms for both officers and enlisted men and a complete hospital. The accommodations could house over 300 men.

The fortress was complete with powerful retractable searchlights and a fire-control station with superb aiming systems. Passageways equipped with both walkways and a narrow gage railway lead from the ammunition depot at the lowest internal level, to where vertical ammunition hoists carried powder and shells up into the gun turrets.

The guns consisted of two 240 mm (9.4 inch) and three 155 mm (6 inch) rapid fire Krupp naval artillery. They were set in well protected fixed bases and the rotatable 12cm (5 inches) thick cupolas looked like enormous turtles on a flat rock.

The main defense perimeter stretched some 6500 meters (4 miles) from the Yellow Sea on the East to Kiaochow Bay on the West. It was constructed on high ground 1200 meters to the east of Bismarck and Iltis forts but lower elevation. The village where the reconnaissance balloons were kept was just inside this defense line a scant 3 miles from downtown Tsingtau.

The defenses consisted of five redoubts with trenches and dug-outs of reinforced concrete. They were built between 1909 and 1913 and were now being modified and strengthened. Each of the redoubts were self sufficient with a bakery, kitchens, generators, ammunition magazines, sleeping quarters, a small hospital, sanitary facilities and other requirements for some 200 men. The area between the redoubts, as well as the flanks were protected by ten blockhouses all interconnected by reinforced trenches, and covered with roofs of iron plates and earth.

From the valley and creek bed all along the front of the line a gradual upward slope had been cleared of all obstacles. Hundreds of trees, pines, oaks, beech, birch and alders were cut down by Chinese coolie work gangs. The logs were saved for covering trenches and for fuel. Barbed wire entanglement were fastened to the stumps. The wire barricades at the entrance to the roads were electrified.

Between here and the redoubts were two reinforced concrete walls 3 feet thick that ran parallel to each other 10 meters apart and 6500 meters long from sea to bay. It was painted white on the side that faced the defenses for the purpose of silhouetting attackers. Black range markers for searchlights and artillery were painted on the walls. Within this "Big Ditch," that was from 5 to 7 meters (16-23 ft.) high, was placed extra heavy multistranded barbedwire secured to pickets made of heavy pointed angle-iron set in concrete blocks. At intervals of about 240 meters were Martello lookout towers, of which about thirty centimeters (1 ft) was visible over the top. The slope continued upward forming the third glacis at the top of which was a parapet of reinforced concrete fire trench. The fire from these trenches swept all three glacis and the wire entanglements. Searchlights, powered by generators, operated with replaceable periscopic mirrors and positioned at strategic locations.

The Germans were able to amass 88 guns and howitzers on the land front in addition to the forts. Most were small caliber, but of the total, 60 were 77 mm or larger and of these 22 were larger than 105 mm. There were dozens of machine gun and look-out posts. The Germans also constructed over twenty decoys from wagon wheels and stove pipes to look like 155 mm cannon only slightly hidden.

Outside the "ditch" there were more wire entanglements

where there were no tree stumps. Five hundred land mines, each weighing 20 to 50 kilograms (44-110 lbs) were buried a short distance further out. The placement was done at night by Germans and not by coolie labor lest they might be tempted by money or physical persuasion to divulge the location to the Japanese.

The Governor approved the razing of two Chinese villages which would obstruct German fire and give the enemy protection. He did refuse permission to destroy two others. Each homeowner was given the equivalence of forty American dollars (a huge sum in those days) and ordered to burn his own house. The Germans then relocated the villagers, as many as they could, into the labor pool. Others fled into Shantung with only what they could carry, begging as they went. The Germans shared what few rations they had with the homeless.

The family of Plüschow's gardener had lived in one of the villages. The flyer noted this "necessary but unfortunate incident" with some regret in his diary, but he was more upset with the leveling of the "beautiful forest that graced the hills."

A poignant anecdotal story was told by Otto Weisinger a non-com reservist and one of the men in charge of cutting down the trees;

"Once, when we wanted to fell a tall tree in a small village, the village elder came to us with tears in his eyes and begged us to save this particular tree. It was his "tree of life" which had been planted by his father on the day of his birth some seventy years ago."

(Co-incidently that was 1844, the year of the beginning of the British "opium wars" against China, who eventually lost trying to keep the foreign narcotics out of the Middle Kingdom.)

"The ginko had faithfully given him shade and long life until now. He was certain that if we should cut down the tree, then he too would not be able to live much longer. We were especially struck by this request because the Chinese do not ordinarily have much understanding of tree cultivation and forest preservation. We gladly acceded to the old man's wishes and he departed gratefully bowing and "chin-chinning," now being convinced that a few more years of his life had been assured him."

The irony of the incident was that only two months later, the Japanese possibly believing the lone tree was left as a German artillery range marker, blew it to pieces with howitzer shells. In fact, that was the rational offered to superior officers questioning why the old man's tree was left standing. It had also been an excellent navigational marker for Plüschow.

The primary water works at Litsun was vulnerable. The secondary reserve pumping station for the city's fresh water supply was located on the north western bank of the Hai-po Creek. Fortified as a strong-point, it was enclosed by the main line of the barb-wire entanglement, but was also vulnerable to attack and bombardment. However, the city had forty wells for back up.

Plüschow, had been diligently fixing possible navigational points on his chart as they made their tour of survey and inspection, escorted by the intelligence officer. Now the officer wanted to drive to the base of Prinz Heinrich a 364 meter high mountain some 6 kilometers (3.7 mi) from the outer defenses. Plüschow had flown over this 1200 foot strategic site and in his subsequent report questioned why there was no observation post situated here. He observed candidly that the location would be far better for directing German fire than the near useless vulnerable "Yellow Sausage." He received a slight rebuke for his choice of words in an official written report, but also praise for his suggestion.

Plüschow;

"The Prinz-Heinrich mountains had a wildly romantic shape, as if they came directly from the moon. It would be easy to defend and very difficult to attack."

Driving east on the dirt road along the coast they stopped in a tiny village at the base of Prinz Heinrich-berg. The open land sloped sharply upwards, scored by vertical ravines called nullahs to where abruptly jagged rocks towered into the sky. One would have to be a mountain climber to reach the summit. The intelligence officer had said it was decided, based on Plüschow's report, that there was going to be an observation post located here. The officer scanned the mountain with his field glasses and compared it to a Takahashi postcard of the mountain. There was a difference. The photo had been altered. The only accessible way to the top had apparently been purposely deleted.

While the OberLeutnant was busy with his tripod mounted camera assisted by the petty officer, Plüschow had time to view the scenery, this time from the ground. When he flew over the mountains he had returned along this same coast and noticed a tiny patch of land 800 meters in diameter connected to the shore by a narrow spit of sand and rocks. It was only an island at the highest tides. This was a "burial island" called Mai-tau by the Chinese. On it were numerous white-washed mud and brick graves built above the ground. The color made them an excellent reference point for aerial navigation.

The hutungs within the village were vastly different from Tsingtau and even the Chinese villages nearer the city. This was the real China, provincial and peaceful. While not far away the frantic preparations for the inevitable naval blockade and land siege made Tsingtau look like a giant ant hill gone mad. Curious children stopped their play of shuttle-cock and cat's cradle to gaze at the foreigners. Two men with wisps of white facial hair growing out of moles sat on small stools in the sun warming their old bones. Each had a song bird within individual bamboo cages with a piece of cuttle-fish bone stuck in it for bill sharpening. They sucked tiny pinches of strong black tobacco in bamboo pipes with brass bowls and stretched their necks to gawk. Two fishermen were launching their heavy sampan by picking up one end at a time and revolving it end-for-end down the beach into the water.

Smells assailed Plüschow's nostrils; the garlicky odor of unwashed bodies; the urine in the gutters; whiffs of hot rancid peanut oil from a food hawker's walking kitchen; rotting fish remains along a creek bank; refuse composting in pig pens, and the human and animal fertilizer spread on the fields by generations of Shantung farmers who have wrested a meager living from the sterile patches of earth in a desperate effort to give back to the land the only thing these peasants could afford and understood that would nourish the soil for yet another growing season.

And there were sounds, some which were familiar to Plüschow, many not. A tinsmith, his shop hanging from a bamboo shoulder pole walked along letting the clanging of metal strips announce to anyone with leaky pots and broken pans that he was available with soldering iron and shears. A smoking charcoal brazier dangled from the rear. A tailor passed with bolts of cloth piled high on his back. He carried a foot pedal sewing machine in one hand and the other twirled a small drum on a stick with a tassel that made the "bunga-bunga" sounds of his profession. A blind man felt his way along a wall and flicked his wrist so a tiny hammer on a leather thong struck a small gong. He also had a begging bowl suspended around his neck. The click of a stick on a hollow bamboo told those behind their walls that a monk was passing. It was good "joss" to drop a few coins into begger bowls. Plüschow would need good luck. He gave them each a copper cash.

Then there was the barking of wonk dogs challenging the strangers and the howls as they were struck by stones thrown by small boys. Chickens cackled as they too were chased. And there was the "Aye-Ho Ah-Ho" chant of coolies moving a heavy load. Plüschow had met China, centuries old, unchanged....but it would not be so for long.

This picturesque hamlet of mud houses with upswept tile roofs and tiny enclosed courtyards was near a small temple on a hill. However it lay on the coast road between Tsingtau and the German garrison at Sha-Tse Kou that was defending the strategic harbor of Lao Shan. The village was directly in the path of the left flank of any attacking force. Plüschow must have wondered if his servant's ancestral home was in a village like this before it was razed.

Because of the prospect of Japanese brutality, many of the German men were worried about their families. Most of the dependents had left by train for Tientsin, but there were still 248 women and children in the city. Meyer-Waldeck issued a proclamation on August 18 for the dependents to leave Tsingtau. Twenty women remained as nurses. A ship, the *Paklat*, had been prepared for just such an evacuation. The Captain had strict orders to stop and not resist if they encountered any hostile naval vessels.

That same afternoon, a few hours from port, five British destroyer torpedo-boats stopped the ship and ordered it to the British protectorate of Wei-hai-wei. They terrified the passengers and crew by practicing dummy torpedo attacks on the vessel and on one occasion a British ship actually struck the German vessel a glancing blow. In port the British seized the ship and held the crew as prisoners of war. The women and children were put aboard a Chinese steamer owned by the British, with a maximum capacity of eighty passengers. The ship only had two toilets. Several days later, after a harrowing trip existing only on bread and water, the ship arrived at Taku Bar in Tientsin. When the news of the uncivilized treatment was received in Tsingtau, the men, for the first time began to understand the realities of war.

Varied methods of communications were established, not only within the military environs of Kiaochow, but with the outside world. A wireless aboard the *Sikiang* a small coastal vessel of the Hamburg-America Line in Shanghai, transmitted all the world's news to Tsingtau. A network of telephone wires were linked between redoubts, lookout posts and fortifications. The rocky terrain did not afford many of the wires to be placed underground, but they could be easily repaired just lying on the surface. There were only three portable two-way wireless sets with a range of only 80 or 100 kilometers, but these were used for special command and control communications in and around Tsingtau. In bad weather, blinker lights, heliograph mirrors, semaphore and even wireless were next to useless. As backup, carrier pigeons were the sole method for transmitting messages.

The first flight path established for the birds was from the lookout post across the mouth of the bay at Cape Jaeschke some eight kilometers seaward from the city. It was a good vantage point to observe enemy ship deployment that could hide behind the islands. Lieutenant Paul Cordau and two men established quarters in a tiny two room deserted yamen (police station) with fifteen carrier pigeons, signal lamps and supplies for a month, including bird seed.

The second observation post, called "Eagle's Nest," was set up atop Prinz Heinrich. There was also a redundant telephone link, signal lamps, heliographic mirrors, and a dozen pigeons. Once situated on the mountain top, the 55 volunteers on this dangerous assignment knew they wouldn't be returning to Tsingtau. They were given special rations of food, cognac and cigars.

Another carrier pigeon link was between Tsingtau and the small fishing village of Tapu-tau west across Kiaochow bay that had a telegraph connection into China. Willys Peck, the American Consul, the only consulate remaining open in Tsingtau, received most of his communiques this way, as did the American Associated Press correspondent. Plüschow was glad he wasn't assigned to the signal corps who was in charge of the carrier pigeons. He was having enough problems with just one bird, the Taube.

When the curfew had been imposed after war was declared, all street lights and exterior land navigational lights were extinguished. Since it was the middle of summer only windows not facing seaward were allowed to be opened, while shutters and shades darkened those facing seaward. Since the cool sea breezes were generally from the south and east, many chose to leave the windows open and not use any lights. Lookouts positioned at Hweichuen fort to the East and from Arkona Island to the south could monitor the blackout. Oil lanterns on rickshaws, horse carriages and carts were turned down or extinguished. Heavy oilpaper, the kind the Chinese used for windows or umbrellas, were used to dim the lights on motor cars and lorrys. The gaily colored paper lanterns festooning beer gardens and alfresco dining areas were not lit. People gathered in the dark to hear the latest news from Germany which were mostly only rumors. Official notices posted each day told of glowing accounts of Germany's victories in Europe. Many optimists believed that the war would be over before it even came to Tsingtau. The pessimists, who claimed they were actually "well informed optimists", believed otherwise.

On August 21, just two days before the Japanese deadline, Captain Meyer-Waldeck held a meeting of all commanding officers.

The Tsingtau Chief-of-Staff, Captain Ludwig Saxer had been in Tientsin on personal business when the mobilization orders arrived. He was the only person who conceived of the idea to get the German artillery smuggled to Tsingtau.

Captain Vollerthun was put in charge of communications. He was Chief of the Kiaochow office for the German Navy in Berlin and had been visiting Tsingtau when the war began.

Lt. Colonel von Kessinger, a strict disciplinarian and not well liked by his men was in command of the land front.

Captain Soldan was in charge of the Engineer Department. Others included the very tall and corpulent Lt. Colonel Kuhlo who was in charge of the German Detachment from Tientsin, and Major Kleeman, Major von Kayser and others.

Each man gave a brief report with assurances that all was ready, at least as well as it could be. Then the Captain gave a brief optimistic but serious speech and wished good luck to everyone. It was a solemn occasion.

That afternoon and the next morning Meyer-Waldeck moved his command post to the Bismarck barracks which was somewhat sheltered by the fortifications on the hill above. He had a spacious reinforced concrete bunker in the basement that would serve as his siege headquarters. The men named it the "ink pot" because of the numerous messages issued from it.

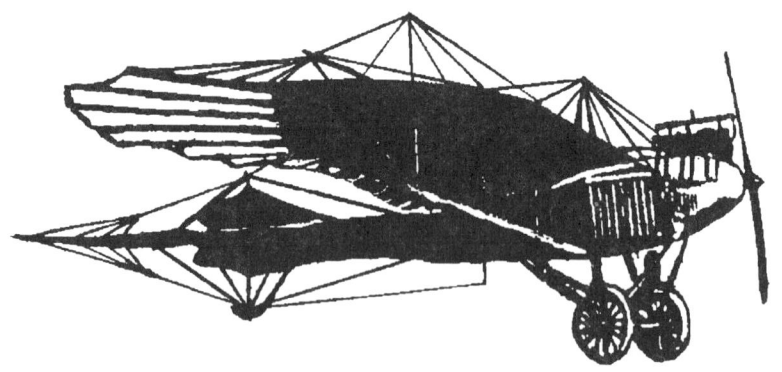

# CHAPTER 5

## BLOCKADE and SIEGE

A mine field had been laid at the harbor mouth and into the Yellow Sea between Lao-shan harbor and the islands south of Cape Jaeschke. On August 22, the day before the expiration of the Japanese ultimatum, the minelayer *Lauting* was sowing some eighty seven mines near the haystack shaped island of Dah Kung-tao 20 kilometers from Tsingtao. The torpedo boat *S-90* was to meet them there as escort. They were not concerned with the enemy, as none had been reported.

At 6:20 p.m. the first salvo fired in the Tsingtau siege was from the British destroyer H.M.S. *Kennet* attacking the *S-90*. Two other British destroyers were on the far horizon also speeding into battle. Although the Japanese deadline was not until tomorrow, the British had been at war with Germany for several weeks.

The German Kapitanleutnant Helmut Brunner steamed at flank speed to warn and protect the *Lauting*. The *Kennet's* first shot went over the *S-90*, the next was a little short, and the third a near miss. The torpedo-boat was deluged with water and the ensign was shredded. Brunner immediately altered course and ordered his gun crews to return fire at will.

The *Kennet* was much larger than the *S-90* and faster, 26 knots. It was in better condition and fired larger guns. But the German had two advantages. It had a low profile and it was in a life or death combat. The engineers were able to deliver a record twenty-two knots. The *Kennet's* larger shells blasted up enormous geysers of water as they missed their swiftly darting target.

It was a clear evening and the sea was like a mirror. The people ashore including Meyer-Waldeck climbed every observation point to view the start of hostilities. Plüschow had just come off duty and was on the veranda of his villa. He had a good vantage point. The sound of the firing from the British ship was described as the deep bark of a bulldog; the German vessel replying with a Dachshund puppy's yelp.

The frantic but accurate firing by the *S-90* did significant damage to the British ship. The Kennet's bridge was hit and six more German strikes put a gun out of action and demolished part of its superstructure. The damaged destroyer doggedly maintained its pursuit. If it could cut the German off from the harbor entrance, the British would win the engagement. The Japanese navy would be sure to "lose face" by the Britisher's first kill. But the *S-90* sped around the rocks of the island to the east. The *Kennet's* Commander, Lieutenant Commander F.A.H. Russel had the unfortunate option of passing the island on the poorly charted west side which he thought could be mined. But to be prudent, he chose to follow the same course as the German and lost the advantage. He was also looking into the setting sun.

The *Lauting*, with eight activated mines still aboard, sped into the harbor entrance. Before either German vessel was hit by the British, a 240 mm shell from Hweichuen fort struck the water near the *Kennet*. The giant geyser made the needed impression. The British destroyer turned abruptly and headed out of range. They had three dead and six wounded, including the commander. The Germans suffered no casualties. The British had fired 300 rounds, the Germans 250.

Noon on August 23 the deadline for a German response to the Japanese ultimatum ran out. It was Sunday and the church services in the morning attracted more than the regular number of worshipers. The Protestants held theirs in the Bismarck Barracks and the Catholics on the Iltis Platz by the aircraft hanger. Meyer-Waldeck attended both services. Immediately afterward the bells of the Christ Church sounded. It was noon.

Plüschow gave the spectators a treat. Just as the bells stopped ringing, he revved the Taube's engine, bumped across the race course and the aircraft ascended somewhat hesitantly to fly a reconnaissance mission. The newly built propeller fashioned by the Chinese carpenters out of oak was not a precise copy of the original. It was 100 r.p.m's slower and couldn't produce as much lift as was necessary. The plane also vibrated more than it did before. He had expected to have his petty officer fly with him as observer, but the extra weight would have been too much. He did climb to 2900 meters directly over Tsingtau so he could observe if any enemy ships were approaching. If there were any, the heat haze concealed them.

That afternoon the Governor had two proclamations distributed throughout the city. The one to the public said in essence, "If the enemy wants Tsingtau, he must come and capture it."

The second message to the military was read at roll-call at Bismarck Barracks:

"On August 15th Japan issued an ultimatum to Germany, in which was demanded the immediate recall of German warships and cruiser squadrons, as well as the unconditional handing over of Tsingtau by September 15. The deadline for reply was noon of August 23....today. This unheard-of demand is insulting in tone as well as in content. We will never voluntarily give up even the smallest piece of land on which flies the German flag. We will not yield from this place, where for the past 17 years we have tried, with devotion and success, to create a small Germany across the sea. If the enemy wants Tsingtau, let him come and try to get it. He will find us at our positions. Therefore we look to the future with confidence, well prepared to meet the enemy."

Meyer-Waldeck also revealed the text of a short message from Germany. It read, "God be with you in this, your difficult struggle. I think of you." (signed) Wilhelm. It was the last dispatch from the homeland.

The terse words from the Kaiser accentuated the exposed vulnerable position of the Tsingtau garrison. They were thousands of miles from home. The Fatherland was at war in Europe with the major powers of France, Russia, and England. Help could not be expected.

A copy of the Japanese Declaration of War, delivered by Viscount Chinda to Robert Lansing, Counselor of the State Department, August 23, 1914, 2 p.m. stated;

"Issued at Tokio (old spelling), August 23, 6 p.m. We by the grace of Heaven, Emperor of Japan, seated on the throne occupied by the same dynasty from time immemorial, do hereby make the following proclamation to all our loyal and brave subjects:

We hereby declare war against Germany, and we command our army and navy to carry on hostilities against that empire with their strength, and we....etc., etc.

Meyer-Waldeck's announcement to his men was less formal. "Today Japan has declared war against Germany!"

There is a letter from Willys Peck the American Consul recently appointed by the President which reads as follows:

*"Dear Myron: In five minutes the period of Japan's ultimatum ends and everyone here expects the Sabbath calm to be slightly shattered, perhaps by the guns of five nations. It is splendid, this waiting. About seven thousand brave men in battery, fort and outpost await for the beginning of a hopeless struggle.*

*The Emperor has telegraphed his wish that Tsingtau shall hold out to the last. And every one is profoundly loyal to that wish. This is just a line to say goodbye during the temporary interruption of communications and to send my love to you and Mary and the children. Always affectionately, (signed) Willys"*

The Japanese Premier's Message to the American people by Count Okuma, August 24, 1914:

*"I gladly seize the opportunity to send, through the medium of "The Independent" (magazine) a message to the people of the United States, who have always been helpful and loyal friends of Japan.*

*It is my desire to convince your people of the sincerity of my Government and of my people in all their utterances and assurances connected with the present regrettable situation in Europe and the Far East.*

*Every sense of loyalty and honor oblige Japan to co-operate with Great Britain to clear from these waters the enemies who in the past, the present and future menance her interests, her trade, her shipping, and her people's lives.*

*This Far Eastern situation is not of our seeking.*

*It was ever my desire to maintain peace, as will be amply proved; as President of the Peace Society of Japan I have consistently so endeavored.*

*I have read with admiration the lofty message of President Wilson to his people on the subject of neutrality.*

*We, of Japan, are appreciative of the spirit and motives that promoted the head of your great nation, and we feel confident that his message will meet with a national response.*

*As Premier of Japan, I have stated and I now again state to the people of America and of the world that Japan has no ulterior motive, no desire to secure more territory, no thought of depriving China or other peoples of anything which they now possess.*

*My Government and my people have given their word and their pledge, which will be as honorably kept as Japan always keeps promises.*——OKUMA."* [Hoover Institution Archives]

For the next several days Plüschow doubled his reconnaissance flights. It was no easy task. He still had to prove the usefulness of his aircraft. Meyer-Waldeck and his command officers still thought the Taube was merely a toy and would probably crash anyway. Benzin was restricted and to save on fuel, after he gained an altitude of two thousand meters, he would cut the motor and glide. He could then observe with his field glasses and write in the log book and study his charts.

The enemy was not in sight. The only troops he saw were the "Mountain Navy Horsemen" on patrol along the border of China and the German territory. To save "horsepower" some patrols pedaled bicycles, which was a struggle on the rutted dirt roads. Flying low over Prinz Heinrich mountain, he waved to the 55 or so men digging in at "Eagle's Nest." They had spent several days climbing up the jagged rocks and dragging their equipment and weapons to the top with blocks and tackle.

After two days of flying Plüschow and his mechanics noticed that the glue in the laminated propeller was separating. It had to again be repaired. It was a miracle it didn't come apart in the air. Now after each flight, the propeller had to be removed and taken to the shops at the dockyard, reglued and put in a press vise until the next flight. Adhesive tape was also stuck along the edges to help keep the wood together. It is interesting to note that only fifty-seven years later, tape was also used to hold the "Moon Buggy" together.

On the early dawn (4:15 a.m.) of August 27, a sailor, Jakob Neumaier, on watch atop Iltis Hill lookout post spotted fifteen vessels on the eastern horizon. Once before in the early morning haze he had given a false alarm and was reprimanded. This time he waited a while and when he was sure, he alerted his superiors.

Plüschow was up early as usual being served coffee on his veranda. He would have been taking off just before sunrise, but again he was grounded because of repairs. He too had sighted the ships through his glasses. The alarm had already been sounded and the shore batteries were on full alert.

Leading the squadron were the Japanese heavy cruisers *Suwo* (the flagship), *Tango* and *Iwami*. The others were destroyers, mine sweepers, cutters and auxiliary supply ships. The British were already on station since "their war" had already started. This included the damaged *Kennet* that was still licking her wounds, three other destroyers and a few auxiliaries. The elderly battleship H.M.S. *Triumph* joined them later. The blockade was assigned to the Japanese second Fleet which consisted of the Second, Fourth and Sixth Squadrons; The Second Torpedo Squadron; The 9th, 12th, 13th Destroyer Flotillas, Auxiliaries and mine sweepers. The First Fleet's Third Squadron would patrol south of Shanghai and the First Squadron would be stationed off the west coast of Korea. The Second and Third Japanese squadron alternated on convoy and blockade duty. The combined strength of the fleet included two dreadnoughts, thirteen predreadnoughts, two battle cruisers, thirteen armored cruisers, twenty-seven torpedo boats, and fifteen submarines.

In addition there were seven gunboats (five formerly Russian); sixteen destroyers; a destroyer tender; a repair-ship; a surveying ship; and converted steamers and other vessels for mine sweeping. Historically the most significant of the vessels was the *Wakamiya Maru* a hydro-plane "mother ship," the first vessel in history to be employed as an aircraft carrier in combat. She carried four Maurice-Farman float planes. The British contribution was the battleship *Triumph*, several destroyers and a hospital ship.

The squadron stopped some 24 kilometers (15 miles) away, well out range. The German gun crews at the four major forts, trained their guns, loaded for maximum range, and waited.

At first, Japanese Vice Admiral Sadakichi Kato sent a radio message asking to meet with Captain Meyer-Waldeck in Tsingtau. The Governor refused, knowing full well what the message would be. He also didn't want the Japanese to observe any military preparedness or weakness. Instead the Vice Admiral had to radio his blockade declaration against the German protectorate to Meyer-Waldeck. The message was in English. A copy was also relayed to the American

Consul W.R. Peck, a neutral and the only foreign consul remaining in Tsingtau. (He evacuated the city five weeks later).

Shortly after the message was received, two Japanese destroyers began shelling Dah Kung-tao and Shao Kung-tao (Big Hay-rock and Small Hay-rock). These tiny islands were uninhabited. The German lighthouse keeper and his wife had been evacuated weeks ago when the beacon was destroyed, as was all the other navigational lights. The brief bombardment was impressive. The Japanese were apparently deceived by the decoy guns of stove pipes and boxes that someone had jokingly set up. Most of the damage was to the cement steps leading to the summit.

When enough shelling had properly celebrated the blockade announcement, two cutters landed marines on the larger island. The Japanese struggled up the very steep "Hay-rock" now without benefit of steps, and planted a Japanese flag. The Germans watching with powerful telescopes even joked that they could see Takahashi taking photos. The Japanese established a look-out post, a wireless station and a navigational light. They were able to report, that on the same day the blockade commenced, they had captured and occupied German territory; the first in World War I, on August 27, 1914 and by the Imperial Japanese Navy!

When the two destroyers ventured too far inshore, one of the big guns on Hweichuen fired a single shell. It was far short, on purpose, but the fifty foot geyser scared away the two vessels. The episode would have been comical had it not been the start of a deadly siege.

The Allied naval operations consisted of steaming just out of range of the guns on Hweichuen Point and firing away at the fort with 10 and 12 inch shells. At first the Germans purposely returned fire at a reduced range. Based on this, and to eliminate the chance for navigational errors, the Japanese anchored a line of buoys just outside the apparent range of the fort, about 15,000 meters or seven and a half miles.

The technique worked well until one day when the Anglo-Japanese commenced target practice they were shocked when a heavy shell hit the British battleship *Triumph* just below her mainmast inflicting casualties and considerable damage which put the vessel out of commission.

There have been reports that at night the Germans moved the buoys within range of their guns. That excuse was apparently circulated so the Japanese could "save face." The truth was that the fort had been firing short so as to lure the Allies closer for the kill. Whichever story was true, the ruse worked.

Having learned the hard way that buoys weren't to be depended upon, the Japanese and British navy extended their range. They elevated their guns beyond the maximum angle by transferring water and fuel (which was coal) to one side thus inclining the ships five degrees. This firing method was inaccurate and did little damage to the German fortifications. The bombardment did render movement outside the forts extremely hazardous.

The Japanese were well aware of the existence of the airfield, but their intelligence had reported that the German planes had crashed and were unusable. The shelling was not aimed intentionally at Iltis Platz even though a few shells landed near the hotel; several didn't explode. The daily number of Allied rounds averaged one hundred and fifty. It was reported that if only three-fourths of the Japanese naval shells exploded upon impact, their firepower would have been substantially more effective.

# CHAPTER 6

## DRAGON MASTER FLIES

The main attack against Tsingtau was by land. The only approach the Japanese could have made, without crossing Chinese soil, would have been at Lao Shan harbor and Sha-tse Kou Bay. But the area was exposed to the weather and for a major landing site the Japanese decided against it for the time being. They would also have to go through a mountain pass in Lao Shan which could have been well defended. Instead they chose to violate the neutrality and sovereignty of China. This didn't seem to concern Japan even in 1914 since they had already conquered Formosa and Korea, won a war against China in 1895 and Russia in 1905 and helped defeat the Boxers in 1900.

The Japanese forces, under command of Lieutenant General Mitsuomi Kamio, landed at Lungkow on September 2, about 300 kilometers north of Kiaochow Bay on the opposite side of the Shantung peninsular entirely in Chinese territory. The information from both couriers and pigeons indicated that the major Japanese force had some twenty-six transports and thirty-six warships in the operation. But this landing was soon learned the hard way to have been a mistake.

Two days before, on August 31st, a severe rain storm lashed the entire area. The Japanese destroyer *Schiratai* ran aground on Lientau Islet just south of Tsingtau. Three destroyers tried to pull the ship clear. They failed, and removed the crew and ship's documents. The storm lessened a bit and Hweichuen fort opened fire with three salvos driving the Japanese vessels away. The gunboat *Jaguar*, of 1898

71

vintage, then ventured out and fired over 100 rounds with her four 15 1/2 pounders at the stranded ship reducing it to a total loss.

The historically unprecedented rain storm lasting for 10 days slowed the Japanese land advance to a near standstill and caused appalling devastation to Shantung province. "Never in remembered or recorded history had so much rain fallen on Shantung province at one time," until now.

Ravines were turned into mountain streams and waterfalls. Dry river beds became roaring torrents devasting everything in its' path. Quiet creeks and rivers overflowed their banks and flooded farmlands and villages. It is estimated that over fifteen times more Chinese perished in these floods than all the casualties on both sides of the Tsingtau siege.

Three German soldiers on reconnaissance were drowned while attempting to cross the swollen Litsun river. These were the first German casualties of the impending siege. Only two bodies were recovered. They were buried in the German cemetary at the north end of Iltis Platz a half kilometer from Plüschow's hanger.

The secondary water-works at Haipo was badly damaged by the flood and Meyer-Waldeck ordered the engineers to begin repairs even in the rain storm.

On September 5, the deluge let up for three hours. Shortly after 10 a.m. an aircraft was heard above the city. At first everyone thought that Plüschow was stupidly flying his Taube in bad weather but Plüschow, working on the plane inside the hanger also heard it. Everyone watched in awe as a bi-winged plane with pontoons gracefully flew over the city. Through field glasses the red circles painted on the wings could be easily seen. The Japanese hydroplane dropped below the low hanging clouds over Bismarck battery. A shiny object fell from the aircraft, whistled loudly through the air and exploded harmlessly in the mud near Bismarck fort making a crater less than a meter wide.

This was the first time in history that true aerial bombs of any significant size were dropped in conflict. Six days before on August 30 a German Taube had dropped a few 3 kilogram 'bombs' (actually explosive devices) on the outskirts of Paris. On November 11, 1911, the Italian pilot Gavotti, flying one of the two Etrich Taubes against Libya, had dropped one pound hand grenades on the Turkish forces at Ain Zara. An American flyer L. Bonney dropped 'explosive devices' weighing only a few pounds on rebel positions for the Mexican Government in 1913. In all instances, the damage was minimal, but the psychological effect of the 14 and 45 pound winged missiles screaming loudly as they fell was terrifying.

This first Japanese flyer/bombardier was 1st Lieutenant Hideho Wada. He survived the Tsingtau campaign and World War II finally retiring with the rank of Admiral. In 1961 he co-supervised the book "Fifty Years of Japanese Aviation 1910-1960."

As translated from the latter; "the plane Wada flew on that first naval air operation in actual war was a Maurice Farman three-seat float biplane that had arrived from France just in time to be loaded aboard the *Wakamiyo Maru* the Imperial navy's first seaplane tender."

Wada, (soon to be promoted to Lieutenant Commander) dropped two more bombs which also did no damage except make the Chinese run like crazy. It was an ineffectual beginning for future Japanese air power, except for the psychological impact on the Germans who now knew the Japanese were serious in their goal. Their bombing might not be effective, but they could conduct reconnaissance missions, scout ship locations, detect mines, and appraise locations for troop landings.

Wada's Maurice Farman was one of four aircraft aboard the *Wakamiyo Maru* that joined the squadron on September 1. The biplane could carry three and was equipped with a simple wireless, bombs improvised from artillery shells and later was fitted with a machine gun. Top speed was 62 mph with a 100 h.p. Renault air-cooled "pusher" engine. (Rear propeller) The length was 32 feet with a wing span of just over 62 feet and the total weight of this massive plane was 2130 pounds. Over one ton! The weight loaded was 3,966 pounds. It had a climb rate of 25 minutes to 1,000 meters (3,281 feet), a service ceiling of 3,000 meters (9,842 feet) and an endurance of four and a half hours. The official naval designation to this plane was Type "Ro-Otsu."

The other three float planes were modified versions of the Maurice Farman, designated Type "Fu" and manufactured at the Yokosuka Naval Arsenal. They were powered by 70 hp air-cooled Renault eight cylinder Vee pusher engines and while the weight was over 500 pounds less, the top speed was only 52 mph. They had a climb rate of 11 minutes to 500 meters (1,640 feet), and an endurance of three hours. All hydros were fitted with two narrow floats without steps, four wheels and two skids for landing giving them an amphibious capability. The 70 horse power engines were not really powerful enough for the double-decker seaplanes as would be soon evidenced when flying against the Taube.

The *Wakamiyo Maru* was built as a naval transport in 1901 and later modified as a sea-plane carrier, Japan's first. It's length of 365 feet and 7600 tons could only travel 9 1/2 knots and it was armed with two 12 pounders. It's single stack and midships's superstructure gave ample room for four large hatches and 4 sets of cargo booms. One plane could be carried fore and one aft each covered with a canvas 'hanger.' the other two aircraft were stowed below, partially disassembled.

The lookouts at Cape Jaeschke reported by carrier pigeon that the ship was anchored in calm waters behind a headland outside the range of the German guns. She could be seen lowering her hydroplanes into the sea, from which they took off and landed. During good visibility the early warning alert of a Japanese air attack was simply a beacon light blinked to signal hill when the Farman flew overhead on the way to Tsingtau. It gave the city about ten minutes notice before the attack.

The next day, when the weather broke again for a few hours, two "evil birds" as the Chinese called them, appeared over the city once more, this time having circled the bay to survey what ships were in harbor. As excitement spread in the city, every German who had a firearm shot at the Japanese planes along with the warships. Even the land artillery joined in. They fired from everywhere, gun emplacements, roofs, windows, the streets, ships and hill tops, with rifles, pistols, and machine guns. Everyone was venting their frustrations.

Once a plane dipped suddenly, rose and dropped again, before leveling off, either through evasive action or turbulence. The thousands of observers cheered thinking the aircraft had been hit. Quickly the pilot climbed higher and circled for his bombing run, this time where he would received little or no gun fire.

The Japanese pilots tried to hit the Taube's hanger with three bombs. None hit their target, but one exploded on a villa near to where Plüschow lived. Fragments flew everywhere, but the two civilian men on the veranda were miraculously uninjured. The only casualties were a number of Chinese wounded from the expended 18,000 bullets, and uncounted artillery and machine gun shells fired at the plane without hitting it. The count came from each man having to give a precise accounting for his own spent rifle ammunition.

FOOT NOTE; (This scenario was reminiscently played out in 1991, but on a much grander scale when Baghdad fired almost as helplessly at the air attacks of Desert Storm.)

After this Meyer-Waldeck ordered an organized warning and anti-aircraft defense. A tall pole was erected on Signal Hill which could be seen by virtually everyone in the city. A large red ball would indicate; aircraft in sight. Two black balls meant; enemy aircraft over the city. Everyone not on necessary work duty must take cover. The Chinese population particularly observed the warning. Most ducked into shelters even when they saw only the single red shape.

The German engineers developed plans for anti-aircraft guns

and built two sets from the *Kaiserin Elisabeth's* rapid firing artillery. Complex firing tables were built, based on mirrors and a range-finding stadimeter, sextant and compass-pelorus. It was suppose to determine the aircraft's speed and altitude with a slide rule vernier providing the needed firing information. This was possibly the first such fire control device used specifically against aircraft.

As long as the aircraft flew in a straight line the system was reasonably effective. However the Japanese pilots had been taught well. They either flew erratically because of intent or most likely, as Plüschow noted in one of his reports, "it was air turbulence that bounced them about." Despite the intensive German attempt, the Japanese never were in great danger from the German anti-aircraft guns. But several times they were seen to be hit, but not fatally. They seemed to be wary of the well fortified harbor area where there were oil storage tanks, the power plant and the mine depot.

Plüschow, realizing the danger of having the aircraft hanger in the open, immediately had a new one built at the other end of the field under a rocky overhang protected by iron plates and completely camouflaged by bamboo matting, green canvas and bushes. Plüschow also had his men build a mock-up plane of bamboo, a wood box, tin, bicycles wheels and canvas. They moved the decoy daily to different positions by the old hanger. The trick was effective. Throughout the siege the German ground crew gleefully watched the Japanese planes bomb the wrong installation.

The Taube was not as airworthy as the Japanese Farmans and he was unable to fly during the rainy weather, not that he could have seen much with such a low overcast. During that period Meyer-Waldeck and his staff had to depend on Chinese spies and carrier pigeons for information, the latter being far more reliable and efficient. Some letters, hidden in hollow bamboo poles, were smuggled out by Chinese couriers. However, these were not important military documents.

The Taube's propeller was still causing problems. In order to get up to speed when taking off to the north where he had to gain altitude to get over the mountains, he would have three over weight reservists hold onto the plane with a rope wrapped around the tail skid. One of the men weighed 135 kilos (nearly 300 pounds). He was well suited for this assignment and probably not any other. The procedure was quite humorous to Plüschow's ground crew. As the engine revved up to speed, the plane would win the comic tug-of-war and the aircraft would gather momentum dragging the obese men down the field until they finally, at Plüschow's arm signal, would let go one end of the rope releasing the plane. Once, the aircraft lifted faster than it should have and two of the men hung on each end of the rope, both afraid to let go. One finally did. The rope came loose and the largest man fell some eight meters to the ground. Only his dignity was injured.

Finally on September 13, Plüschow took off for an early morning extended reconnaissance mission in search of the enemy. He flew inland skirting the bay to Liu-ting, then crossed the still rapidly flowing White Sand River at the border and into China heading a little west of north.

The bad weather that flooded the country had turned roads into muddy quagmires and made the Japanese change their tactics. The landing on the north coast was halted on September 3. Some of the troops re-embarked and the ships re-deployed for a landing at Lao-Shan and Wo-ko Tschuang Bay closer to Tsingtau but still in Chinese owned territory.

The several thousand men, arms, supplies and horses already ashore spent the next two weeks advancing only 220 kilometers against no opposition except the weather and terrain. Struggling across swollen streams that turned into raging rivers, and through thick mud the men and horses were exhausted from eighteen hour a day forced marches.

After an hour's flight, Plüschow was nearly half way across Shantung province. Flying only a few hundred meters above a small hill near Pingtu, he found Japanese troops and cavalry floundering along a muddy road and struggling with supply wagons, and artillery caissons. When they spotted him, the foot soldiers immediately broke into two lines and remained frozen as if in a drill exercise. As he flew overhead, they quickly leveled their rifles and fired volley after volley in sequence almost by the countdown. Plüschow pulled back on the controls to gain altitude, but the sluggish Taube with the makeshift propeller struggled to reach 1500 meters. But this was not high enough. He climbed to 2000 meters. The Japanese continued their rhythmic firing pattern that was not unlike the effect of a machine gun. He heard the bullets whistle past him, but no critical parts of the craft or pilot were hit. Later he discovered several holes in the plane. He learned to respect his enemy after experiencing the unique small arms anti-aircraft fire.

Plüschow kept above two thousand meters. He was a hundred kilometers from Tsingtau and his return flight took him over the walled city of Tsimo. He climbed to three thousand meters to get over the mountains of Lao Shan, to reach the sea. There was no indication of any Japanese landing force. Then he headed back down the coast flying low enough to wave at the garrison at Shat-tse kou bay. Passing over the white graves on "burial island" he sighted the Japanese warships in the distance beyond the "Hay Rocks." They had suspended the bombardment and were just maintaining the blockade. He counted and logged them for his report.

When he landed at the airfield in mid morning, Plüschow had flown over 240 kilometers (150 miles). Because of the reduced propeller revolutions, the Taube's top speed had been reduced from 69 miles an hour to about 58, cruising speed was even lower. The entire flight had taken slightly over two and a half hours.

Up to this time his superiors and the general staff paid little or no attention to what Plüschow did or said. He decided to file his written report the next day as usual. He spent the afternoon patching ten holes in the plane, regluing the propeller and overhauling the engine.

Plüschow's diary;

"At the beginning, the staff officers didn't think much of my plane, nor of aviation in general. But soon it all changed! That same evening, by coincidence I went to Government House to see a friend. There I met the Chief of Staff who was in a hurry since he had left an important meeting with the Governor to get some documents. In passing he cried; "Well Plüschow, have you been flying in your motorized kite?"

"Yes sir," I replied, "I just returned. I surveyed inland, saw troops at Pingtu, but nothing of the enemy along the coast."

I can still remember the surprise on the face of my superior. "What! You flew along the coast and you only now tell me? We have been meeting for two hours discussing how to defend against the large troop landings which was reported today by our spy. And you just casually come in here and give me such an excellent report! Hurry, to the Governor!

The report from a Chinese mercenary spy had been a lie! My Taube and I were finally recognized as an important part of the military intelligence and the defense of Tsingtau."

# CHAPTER 7

## ANGLO / JAPANESE
## AIR-SEA-LAND SIEGE

The "Dragon Master" had brought back the first concrete eyewitness information concerning enemy movements, location and strength. Now that Plüschow had proven that air reconnaissance could be a valuable asset to military operations, he was now included in Meyer-Waldeck's staff meetings.

Obviously, from the flyer's report, the Japanese, despite the bad weather conditions, were moving considerable forces, including artillery across Shantung. The weather that had been on the side of the Germans, had now cleared. The Japanese would soon be at the edge of German territory. The weakness in the German intelligence and communication system was confirmed by the Japanese being able to march half way across the province undetected and unreported by Chinese spying for the Germans.

It was obvious that the Japanese forces would establish headquarters in Tsimo, a walled town of some 15,000 people, a mere 40 kilometers north of Tsingtau. From this location the logical approach was through Liu-ting across the Pai-sha ho (White Sand River) then across rolling farmlands of gaoliang (millet), sweet potatoes, and peanuts. The Japanese would have to struggle through the hilly terrain through the villages of Tsau-Yuen, Tsan-kou, and Litsun.

The railroad was unusable. The moving stock had been sabotaged, several bridges demolished, and a section of track carried away. If they stayed on the road nearest the Bay, the ships could shell their approach. At this point the Germans might present a concentrated defense and stop the Japanese, but not indefinitely. The orders were to hold the enemy as long as possible, then "March Backwards."

The other possible route for an advance was on the Japanese left flank. This would take them through the mountain pass of Hotung, by way of the Mecklenburg House, a health spa and spring to Marsch Pass. This was a difficult, steep single-file mule trail as was Kletter Pass, the only other way through. The Germans didn't believe the Japanese would cross the mountains here, which could be well defended.

This certainty of the General Staff concerning the Japanese approach collapsed when Chinese agents reported that off Lao Shan Bay there were Japanese ships. As there were only three cargo vessels and a few warships, Meyer-Waldeck did not believe that with so few vessels, a substantial Japanese amphibious landing was possible. After the previous false alarm by the Chinese spies, who probably got paid for each report, this last story could only be verified by air reconnaissance.

The next day Plüschow confirmed that not only was the Chinese report true, but he had observed the smoke of numerous freighters and warships approaching from the north east. The weather was exceptionally clear. Plüschow had ascended laboriously to 3200 meters and estimated that the fleet was about 130 kilometers distant, half the length of the Shantung peninsula. The smoke from coal burning vessels of that era made it difficult to hide their location.

Shortly before dawn on September 18 the Japanese initiated their landing on Chinese territory just south of the village of Wang-ko Chuang north of Lao Shan Bay. Just before the troop transports arrived, six battle cruisers bombarded the hills and terrain around the landing site to preclude any resistance from the Germans. Over 28,000 men, tons of equipment, 290 horses and over 140 siege cannon would eventually be landed.

Major Kihara from the Imperial General Staff had, a few days previously, investigated the area. On his first visit he and a companion, with only side arms, were nearly captured by the Germans. They barely managed to escape in their small boat under heavy rifle fire. The next day they returned, this time with a machine gun. They drove the Germans back and retired properly having "saved face." This experience showed the Japanese that the Germans were present and would resist.

Kihara described the landing area as a broad shelving beach with a good rise and fall of tide. Just inland was an expanse of flat ground for storing guns, ammunition and supplies and for exercising horses. The ground was suitable for starting the roadbed for a light railway along the relatively flat coastline. But more important, the bay would allow anchorage of several scores of vessels. The Japanese established a beachhead without resistance and immediately deployed scouting parties into the mountains.

The First Company commanded by a Captain Kamaji, quickly marched toward Hotung Pass. It was eight kilometers from the landing beach and estimated to be about ten kilometers from the Germans. The path was narrow and rugged, no wider than a tight double file of soldiers. The rugged mountains towered steeply above them. After a difficult climb they were about 700 meters from the top of the pass when they received German fire. The men were in well sheltered trenches with gun ports on higher ground.

There were forty defenders under the command of Lieutenant Gunther Below. He was a high school teacher in Tsingtau and an avid hunter and a excellent marksman. He was itching to fight, but his orders were to delay, rather than block the enemy.

Kamaji divided his company into thirds. One third would engage the Germans in a fire fight. The others he sent over the crags and precipices to out-flank the defenders. When they finally coordinated their attack they found the Germans had already departed. Both sides had each fired about 500 rounds. No casualties were reported.

With the pass secured, the Japanese could now off-load their men and supplies and advance into German territory unrestricted. One Japanese company slipped quietly into the tiny village of Tu-lau just inside the protectorate, and routed a half dozen surprised Germans who didn't fire a shot. These were the first Japanese soldiers who stepped foot on captured German territory in World War I; it was September 19, 1914. The Imperial navy had preceded them by several weeks by occupying several small undefended offshore islands and gained much prestige.

Each time Plüschow would submit his reports to both the 'Ink-Pot' and Government House, he would read the latest news bulletins. Many now included his observations. Some could have been propaganda. But in the light of later well documented Japanese atrocities during the Sino-Japanese war between 1937 and 1945 these 1914 reports must have an excellent basis of fact.

NEWS BULLETIN Tsingtau, September 20, 1914

*"The reports of robberies by the Japanese advance guard are increasing. Repeatedly it is reported that they confiscate cattle, fowls, provisions and vehicles without paying a cent for them. Chickens are slaughtered in the streets. Locked houses are forced open; women are being raped. In the bay of Wang-ko-chuang the Japanese seized three sampans full of pears without payment. The fruit and Chinese crews were taken aboard Japanese ships and the sampans were set adrift. On account of these robberies and extortions, the Chinese are greatly incensed.*

*It is also confirmed that numerous Chinese robbers (bandits) are among the Japanese troops. Of the 130 horsemen who appeared in Tsimo, there were only 45 or 50 Japanese; the others being Chinese, Koreans, Hunghutzus; in short, all sorts of riff-raff. The leader is a Tsimo man, who formerly was sentenced in Ta-pu-tau for gambling and opium smoking and dealing and who was known as an active revolutionist in Chefoo. As a man acquainted with the country, he acts as a scout. Like his men, who are known as scoundrels, he wears a Japanese uniform. With such people Japan is conducting its "friendly war." To a cultured nation, which Japan wants to be, this is disgraceful. But the veils are lifting from Japan as well as from her ally, Great Britain, the latter having betrayed the white race!"*

On September 15, Japanese riders, dressed in Chinese civilian clothes with their rifles hidden amongst bundles of firewood, tried to infiltrate the German defense line north of Liu-ting. They were driven back. The horses gave them away. They were not the small native Mongolian ponys prevalent in the area, but tall Arabians. Skirmishes occurred all along the perimeter of the protectorate. Mostly the Japanese were probing the defenses and testing the will of the Germans to defend territory so far from Tsingtau.

The first real defeat of the Japanese occurred when they occupied Kletter pass in the thirty five hundred foot mountains of Lao Shan. They assumed they were secure in their lofty position, and believed that the German refusal to engage them was permanent. On September 23, Major Ander attacked the Japanese from below with 130 men, 4 machine guns and 2 pieces of artillery. Outflanking them in a furious fire-fight and using all his weapons, Major Anders overran the Japanese who fled in disorder. The action that lasted two hours had two wounded on each side. The Japanese "lost much face."

Among the spoils of the battle were tents, food packs and several rifles. The Germans also found postcards and photographs taken by Takahashi. These were of various strategic areas around Tsingtau. Later when the Japanese characters on the back were translated, it read, "Future new address of T. Takahashi: Friedrick strasse, Tsingtau." While the fire-fight was not an important one, it did boost the morale of the Germans. As it has been from time immemorial, the war stories told of exaggerated enemy casualties and extensive captured booty.

When the token contingent of Britishers (eventually a brigade force of four battalions) arrived at Laoshan Bay on September 22, there was fifty seven warships and transports at anchor. A long floating jetty had been built onto which the small vessels could unload men and supplies. Large iron pontoon barges were used to carry the huge howitzers and naval cannon ashore. A huge floating heavy-lift crane was employed to off load the heavy weapons and equipment. The Japanese also commandeered several hundred large sampans that they used to off-load supplies and men from the transports. Some 650 large wheel barrows were also forced into service along with their owners, usually two men to each barrow. Over 600 two wheel pony carts were impressed into service. They couldn't carry much weight, but could travel the bad roads with relative ease. Diesel generators were powering searchlights so work could continue throughout the night.

A narrow gage Decauville railway was being laid to Litsun. It was described by J.A. Irons, one of the U.S. military observers in U.S. Army Military Research Collection dated February 23, 1915.

"It arrived in sections consisting of two light rails bolted to about nine flat iron ties. Virtually anyone could assemble them when placing them on a roadbed. The roadbed required little work beyond smoothing, but it did require adjacent walking space for the men assembling the railway. Each car was flat 1 x 1 meters and light enough to be lifted without difficulty. During construction each car carried at least four track sections. As the men emplaced these sections, they moved the car forward until it was empty. Then they simply lifted it off the rails and placed the car to one side. When all the subsequent cars were empty, they quickly put them all back on the rails and hurried them back for more loads. The cars had hand-operated brakes, which allowed easy control on down grades. The readily available Chinese conscripted laborers permitted construction without extensive Japanese manpower losses. As they planned a construction rate of eight miles per day, the Japanese moved an average of 300 flat cars with 150 tons of material each day."

The British were surprised to find the beach master's tent displaying the Japanese rising sun flag and the British Union Jack flying from crossed poles. The Japanese were well organized.

The battalion (800 men) of the 2nd South Wales Borderers disembarked within two days. A battalion of Indian Sikhs would arrive later. Colonel (Acting Brigadier General) N.W. Barnardiston and his forces were under the command of Lieutenant General Kamio the Japanese commander in chief. This was the first time in history that Western troops were commanded by Asiatics. The British were ordered to join the Japanese army on the right flank south of the walled city of Tsimo to the west.

Barnardiston's request to be on the attacking left flank by the sea was denied politely by Kamio. The British had wanted to be closer to their hospital ship if needs be. There was no doubt as to who was the Commander-in-Chief. On September 25, the British started their march of more than 48 kilometers over a narrow muddy road shared with Japanese infantry and vehicles. There was a vast difference between the march discipline of the British to the Japanese. The latter would straggle along in broken columns, stop at will to smoke, eat, rest or relieve themselves.

The Japanese asserted their assumed superior role by breaking into the British columns marching "ever so properly" and driving the men into the muddy fields. The long vines of sweet-potatoes slowed their progress. Mud was over their puttees and up to their tropical shorts. They had just come from Wei-hai-wei still wearing their summer clothing. Their warm uniforms and food supplies had not yet arrived. The men were on half rations, and depending on the charity for Japanese provisions. Tempers and ill-will between the "Allies" were more intense than against the German enemy.

The bodily hygiene between the two races were markedly different. The Japanese valued personal cleanliness and distrusted anyone with body odor. It is documented that before World War 2, "a man with strong body odor could be rejected from the military because it showed he was of bad character". Because it was so uncommon, that was the reason the Japanese had such a strong aversion to body odor. But while the Japanese were scrupulously clean with their body; constantly washing in the streams and creeks, they left their toilet droppings in the open. The British, on the other hand, would bury their offal, but bodily bathing was a rarity. It was said "they would almost rather cross a mine field than where the Japanese did their toilet." While the British considered the Japanese "coolie soldiers" as inferior, the Japanese considered the unwashed British as "smelly barbarians."

The British soldiers could hear the sound of guns trading artillery fire and see the Japanese planes circling over the lines of battle. In the distance were the masts and smoke stacks of the German warships. All these sights and sounds heightened them with the prospect of engaging the enemy.

In order to present himself to his superior, Lt. General Kamio, Barnardiston had to travel to Liu-ting, where the Japanese were setting up an advance command post. When he crossed the border over White Sand River, he was the first Britisher during World War I to enter German territory, if only briefly.

Kamio was gracious in his meeting with the Englishman. Throughout the interview Kamio maintained a dignified aloofness but he revealed no military plans. It was like he treated the British presence as merely observers. Barnardiston departed without accomplishing much except receiving verbal orders that he had to proceed to the town of Li-tsun 10 kilometers from the German main line of defense. His task was to capture and hold the water-works.

Lieutenant General Mitsuomi Kamio had risen through the ranks to command positions. Having served in Europe as a military attache, he spoke English and German reasonably well. Approaching his sixtieth birthday and sporting a heavy white moustache, he was a leader that inspired confidence. He had much practical experience and was attentive to details. With Kamio there would be no fool hardy adventurous campaign, but with him in command there was no doubt as to the outcome. Kamio knew what and who the opposition was as he stated in a short address to his men.

"The German army is considered the best in the world. Our 18th Division is going to represent the entire Japanese Army. Now is the time for us to demonstrate wariness, courage and energy."

The Japanese had tried to emulate the excellence of the German military and actually accepted many of them as instructors in Japan. Many on both sides used to be friends, now enemies.

Japan would have enlisted the tutorage of German aviators, except that Imperial Germany's military in 1912 and 1913 had little regard for aviation. The eager Japanese enlisted the help of the more progressive French. They bought and used and copied their Maurice Farman aircraft which were far better suited for military use than the Tauben (pl) Germany was using at the start of the war.

By December of 1914 the German Tauben were relegated to only training purposes. The axiom of the early German Taube pilots were that you had to be good to fly an "untethered kite with a motor."

Kamio, from the "old military school," was not completely trustful of Japanese aerial intelligence reports. And the brief land reconnaissance skirmishes brought little information as to the German strength except that they were resisting all along the front, and they were good marksmen. One particular skirmish, well documented, was particularly poignant and almost humorous.

On September 18, while the Japanese were stalking the Germans in the tall soybean and gaoliang (millet) fields across the river from Liu-ting they gave their position away by accidently firing a rifle shot. A fire-fight broke out between the combatants.

The much smaller German patrol retreated into the fields, the Japanese after them. Suddenly twenty more German infantrymen on their flank began firing. After twenty minutes of heavy shooting Captain Suida Sakuma, was hit, by a "stray" bullet, so the Japanese reported. A chest artery was punctured and he died quickly, the first man killed in the Tsingtau land action.

Because of the superior force, the Germans began retreating. As they were "backward marching", one of their officers, Baron von Riedesel fell, shot through both legs. He ordered his men back as he protected their withdrawl. He was an excellent shot and caused enough casualties among the Japanese to stall their attack. Later a few Germans returned and found he had bled to death, but not before he had written a brief goodby note to his wife in Peking.

As documented by "Weltkrieg," page 45, Hanyu:

"Both men were well liked and respected by their men. Sakuma, a simple man who exemplified Japanese military virtues, avoided hard liquor and honored his Samurai ancestors was mourned by many. The same was true of Baron Riedesel, a reservist, who had been First Secretary in the German diplomatic embassy in Peking. His selfless action was in character."

Documented by Uhlenhuth, "Tsingtau Tagebuch," 17-18 September 1914:

"One of the eerie, unreal aspects of this small drama was the behavior of the Chinese. In Liu-ting a colorful wedding procession with drums, gongs and flags moved through the street, the gaily dressed participants proceeding on their way irrespective of the flying bullets.

In the fields the farmers kept at their work until the bullets came too close, when they would take cover for a few minutes, and then stolidly returned to their labors."

The Japanese always tried to recover their dead or wounded. Once when they were retreating from their defensive position and out gunned by the Germans they hastily tried to put their wounded onto the horses. A German eyewitness, Otto von Gottberg wrote;

"The more seriously wounded comrades, which they could not move onto the horses, were killed in front of our eyes. But not as you might expect by a merciful shot, but with their swords."

"After the Japanese fled we found one soldier still barely alive. He died when we tried to remove him. It was now evident that the enemy would not let any of their men be taken prisoner.

Nearly all the Japanese officers, who faced capture, killed themselves by a shot from their pistol. This is not incomprehensible. One reason is that the Japanese learned from us and they didn't want to face the double shame of the student not measuring up to the standards of the master instructor."

The real reason is that the ancient Bushido mentality is deeply ingrained in the Japanese warrior.

The regiment of the Japanese 22nd Cavalry consisted of 290 sword wielding horsemen and were headquartered at Liu-ting. The cavalry engagements between the two sides were much different than that portrayed by the Japanese illustrated posters printed and circulated back home during the siege. For one thing the posters didn't show the short Japanese looking ludicrously small atop large and beautiful Arabians, now muddy and exhausted from the long overland trek. The tall Germans, on the other hand astride tiny Mongolian ponies with their boots nearly dragging the ground, looked equally ludicrous. But in the rough terrain these hardy ponies could outrun and outlast the Japanese mounts.

The Germans, in order to camouflage the white ponys, used a solution of potassium supermanganic potassium chlorate to stain their coats a soiled-yellow khaki color. The objection to this practice by the lone German veterinary doctor was not heeded.

To conserve their ponies, the German cavalry would also use bicycles to patrol when the muddy roads were passable. The Japanese cavalrymen attacking the German "bicycle cavalry" must have been unique. On one occasion, the Germans, when they had to "march backwards," just sabotaged the bicycles, left them in the peanut fields and retreated.

War stories of varied interest were circulated throughout the city. This one occurred at the outpost near the village of Ai-Erl-Tien. Around three in the morning, when dawn was just beginning to break, the first peasants were already arriving with heaped wheelbarrows and baskets suspended from shoulder poles, full of farm produce to be sold in Tsingtau that same morning. All incoming Chinese were allowed to pass freely, while those going out were throughly searched. This seemed a curious order. Just how thoroughly one sometimes has to search in the interest of military security is apparant from the story that the eye witness Wiesenger related.

"One fine day when I was on field-watch duty, my comrade and I saw a Chinese woman riding towards us on a donkey which was led by a young boy. They passed through the opening in the wire entanglement at the road block. In itself, this was not a very unusual occurrence, but the fact that the rider was wearing a brand new outfit, consisting of a dark blue "Skirtblouse" (E-Shang) and a pair of bright red trousers. Ordinarily one would not wear ones best clothes for a dusty ride. Our special attention was aroused.

Her features were smooth and even. The Tai-Tai, as the Chinese women are called, usually had rather old and ravaged faces. My comrade mentioned that he was a bit suspicious of this passer-by. He further thought it strange that a young boy should be leading the donkey, as this was the duty of the husband. Too much time had passed when we came to realize that it might have been a disguised Japanese agent. We were unable to do anything but determine to watch out more carefully the next time.

We didn't have to wait long. Again the next day a Tai-Tai appeared on her donkey with a little girl at her side. She had a strikingly fresh and youthful appearance. While her clothing was not quite so conspicuous, it seemed to us that, for Chinese standards, her figure was too plump and stocky.

When she came closer and we looked at her severely, she shyly averted her eyes and tried to conceal her face. This was enough for us to make her stop and dismount. We tried to make her comprehend, in German and Chinese, that we took 'her' to be a disguised Japanese man. It was odd that this person did not seem to want to understand us properly. We therefore took her to the officer on duty in the guard house.

After much commotion and womanly shrieks, the embarrassed officer told us that he had established, beyond a doubt, that we were dealing with a real Tai-Tai!"

Of course the query, asked by more astute listeners of the tale at the Furstenhof Beer Garden was; "How do you know that she wasn't a Japanese woman spy?"

On September 25, the Japanese were ready for a major push into German territory from Liu-ting on the right flank, Lao Shan harbor on the left and over the mountain passes in the middle. The narrow gage "Decauville" railway had been built starting from the beachhead near Lao-shan Bay and was still being extended to key positions along the front. Howitzers and field artillery and supplies were constantly arriving on the efficient little rail system. A few days previous, the Japanese had initiated a landing at Sha-tse Kuo Bay and successfully captured the German outpost. It was not like depicted in the Japanese propaganda illustration showing a major assault and landing.

This garrison of some 50 men had positioned themselves at this strategic outpost at the offset of hostilities. The men were relegated to live in tents while the officers moved into an old custom's post. The local customs agent was a former pirate with some knowledge of German. He entertained them with numerous "sea-stories" of his experiences. The officers were nearly eaten alive by the mosquitoes. The men and non-coms wisely moved to a nearby Chinese temple for relief after paying "Kumshaw" to the Abbott. Extra burning of incense kept the ravenous mosquitoes at bay.

On September 14, the day before the torrential rain storm, the Japanese torpedo boats swept into Sha-tse-kou bay fired a quick bombardment for several hours and fled before the Germans could respond. Plüschow had been surveying the area by car and was caught in the shelling.

"I drove by car to Schatsy-kou where the advance posts were located. Without being aware of any danger, I stopped in front of the command house. To my surprise, all the officers and troops lay on a protected slope that rose toward the sea and waved frantically to me. I believed it to be a salute and waved back. I was still in my car when I heard a whistling sound above my head. Then an explosion. Only ten steps away, the first grenade (exposive shell) exploded. Before I could think twice, the next ones landed in quick succession. I ran out of the car to the others and their questionable cover.

Above the rise, I could see what was happening. A Japanese torpedo-boat flotilla was attacking Schatsy-Kou by gun fire. We were pinned down for two hours without seeing anything, without adequate cover and without moving under their grenade attacks. No one was injured. Then it must have been lunch time for the Japs because they stopped firing.

When we inspected the damage to the house and the area, small Chinese boys were already collecting grenade fragments. Soon after, as we were sitting down to a cup of coffee, three small pigtailed boys came in happily holding in their dirty little fingers three blind grenades (unexploded shells) which they threw calmly onto the table. If they had exploded it would have been an exciting party!"

When it became evident that the outpost could not be effectively defended, Kessinger ordered the men to evacuate to Litsun. After blowing up what was left of the mosquito-ridden customs house, destroying two cannon and burying two machine guns, the Germans silently abandoned the important defensive outpost without firing a shot. It was NOT under fire or enemy pressure as the Japanese reported and depicted in their illustration or even as several authors stated, most notable of whom was the German writer Vollerthun in 'Der Kampf um Tsingtau.'

Kamio's estimation that a 2000 man well-positioned force opposing him made him extra cautious, as did the reports of the German military successes in Europe. Actually there were only 700 Germans on the entire 40 kilometer front, but concentrated in the west. The Germans were as ready as they ever would be to resist the Japanese. The orders were to hold the enemy as long as possible while "marching backwards."

The warships *S-90* and the *Jaguar* were deployed to the northern part of Kiaochow bay just off the town of Tsang-kou on the main rail line, now in Japanese hands, albeit unusable.

The Japanese had a good idea where the German defenses were positioned. A few days previously on September 21, the Japanese Army Air Corp. had arrived at Tsimo. Prior to that all the Japanese air activity was mainly conducted over the city by the navy. Now the army had eyes in the sky. Under the command of Lt. Colonel Yoichi Arikawa (later Lt. General), it comprised of four Maurice Farman 1913 machines powered by Renault 70 hp air-cooled Vee engines. They had almost the same characteristics as the navy planes except they had only wheels. The maximum speed was 90 km/h (55.9 mph) with an endurance of four hours. There was also a French Nieuport N.G.2 monoplane. Powered by a Gnome 100 hp air-cooled rotary radial, the two seater had a maximum speed of 110 km/h (68.4 mph) and an endurance of four hours.

The Lungkou Army air field near Tsimo was only 30 minutes flying time from Tsingtau. Flying from the hastily constructed field the Japanese soon located the German troop positions and defenses.

The Germans were unable to shoot down any of the planes, but their fire power kept the Farmans above 2,000 meters, (about 6500 feet). The Japanese aircraft conducted aerial surveillance regularly.

With a pilot and an observer in each of one or two planes, they would fly over the German lines, make notes, draw positions on maps and drop the information on clip boards tied to streamers onto Kamio's headquarters. This method of intelligence gathering was the accepted method at the birth of military aviation. Lt. Wada, however, had a two-way wireless to relay intelligence and fire-control reports to the navy. Even with the dots and dashes of the Morse code, this method of communications was the state-of-the-art.

The Japanese aircraft had determined that the Germans had three defense lines. The first was merely a system of outposts that ran along defensible territory, but not manned with enough men. Kamio knew they proved no obstacle to his troops even though his men were being killed and wounded by German marksmen. The second line stretched from Kiaochow Bay to Waldersee, the mountain next to the "Eagle's Nest." This was an irregular series of fortified positions. The air surveillance had also revealed that this was the strongest area available to the Germans, but again beyond their resources of equipment and men. Behind it was the "big ditch" and the main land fortifications in front of the city.

The Japanese also employed photography for air surveillance. It could have been very logical that Takahashi, the Tsingtau photographer and spy, was on hand to evaluate the aerial photos, although there is never a record of Japanese covert intelligence activity.

Kamio had an aversion to written orders. Even at a staff meeting he would give orders, have an officer that he picked at random, to repeat them and then dismiss the group. The British Brigadier found this very disconcerting even if one of his officers, Lieutenant Colonel Calthrop, spoke fluent Japanese.

Plüschow was now well aware of the existence of the nine Japanese aircraft. He was also ordered not to engage in any foolhardy stunts that would endanger the lone Taube. Daily flights, made at Plüschow's discretion, became routine. But he was still plagued with technical problems. After every few hours of flying, the laminate of the propeller had to be reglued and retaped. Plüschow knew full well the possibility that if it came apart in the air, he would at best crash land behind enemy lines. At this early period of flying, parachutes were not used, even if available. The Taube could glide a considerable distance like the dried Zanonia seed it was patterned after. That was one of the reasons for flying high along with being invisible from the ground.

Watanabe, in command of the artillery, suggested that most of the setting up of heavy guns and emplacements should take place only at night and the positions camouflaged during the day when the German plane was flying. However this would delay the scheduled completion. His respect for Plüschow exceeded that for a full German regiment. He saw the German flyer as a fundamental threat to Japanese success. To aid Watanabe, Kamio ordered his air force to keep the German 'sky spy' away. The former nuisance had grown into a problem. However with the Taube's invisibility above 1500 meters, the Japanese often could not tell if he was airborn.

Up to now the Japanese had been able to advance almost unimpeded. There had been skirmishes, but no intensive resistance. But once they got to the hills of Tsang-kou they were slowed. During daylight, from both ships and land, the Japanese came under heavy artillery fire. From atop Prinz Heinrich Mountain, the Germans directed their ground fire by telephone to the land batteries and with heliographic mirrors and signal lights to the warships with moderate success.

In the bay the *S-90* the *Jaguar* and the venerable cruiser *Kaiserin Elizabeth*, deployed to the northeastern part of Kiaochow Bay, intensified their firing at the enemy, and inflicted casualties. The advancing troops could only move safely at night. The advance was being bogged down.

As counter measures against the warships that were hampering troop movement along the advancing right flank, the Japanese sent their army aircraft on a bombing mission on October 4. This was a definite snub against their own Naval Air Force. It was also to be the first air-sea military engagement in history.

# CHAPTER 8

## ONE FLYER AGAINST NINE

The following extracts are from the Japan Weekly Mail of October 21, 1914; "AN OFFICIAL STATEMENT MADE BY THE WAR DEPARTMENT YESTERDAY AFTERNOON IS AS FOLLOWS:"

*"One monoplane and two biplanes of our Aviation Corps left their base the morning of the 27th, (Sept) and bombed the enemy's vessels to the west of Tsangkow. They threw many bombs from an altitude of from seven to eight hundred metres."*

*The report went on to say that the missiles hit the vessels or exploded close to them. Several of the Japanese planes were admittedly hit by shell fire, but there were no casualties and all returned safely. The attack was noted as being a great success.*

*German reports and other historical documents confirmed that no German warship was ever "badly" hit by Japanese aerial bombs during this campaign. Paraphrasing a German report; "The three warships constantly maneuvered evasively and kept up heavy fire at the advancing ground troops. The Japanese flyers soon learned that the ships could easily dodge their bombs. The planes would attack with the sun at their backs and would have to dive to about 650 meters before dropping their bombs. Just as the planes would make their turn for the straight run, the ships would swerve hard to starboard or port and the bombs would miss, sometimes by not much."*

During the first day of the air-sea battle, the anti-aircraft fire from the ships shot between 15 and 30 machine gun bullet holes in the three planes used in the attack, but none were shot down and there were no casualties. Despite the heavy resistance, the Japanese made numerous bombing attacks on the ships for several more days with little or no effect, except for near misses. While the planes didn't substantially damage the ships, their dodging maneuvers hampered their gun fire against the Japanese land targets.

It is interesting to note that the Japanese Army Air-Corps bombs, consisting of artillery shells with attached fins, weighed between 14 and 45 pounds. If they had struck a vessel they would have caused considerable damage. During the attack on Pearl Harbor 27 years later, the Japanese battleship *Nagato's* 16-inch armor-piercing shells weighing 1,760 pounds were specially modified to be dropped as bombs. Both Japanese and American historians believe that one of them sank the battleship *Arizona*.

A more serious danger to the naval forces came, not from the planes, but from the Japanese artillery. At first they didn't score any hits, but soon the deck plates were covered with water and iron fragments from near misses. Then the *Jaguar* was hit on the bow causing some damage but no casualties. This exchange of shells provided a good deal of noise, but it was nothing to the sound of the land artillery duel. The first day of the major attack, the Japanese suffered heavy losses. Once when masses of infantry were fording the Li-tsun river with horse drawn artillery caissons, the Germans held their fire until the enemy was mid stream. Then Bismarck Fort opened up with their 280 mm cannon. Two direct hits decimated hundreds of infantry. Other shells landed among the men on the far bank waiting to cross, also causing heavy losses. The men retreated in confusion.

They were under observation from the spotters on Prinz Heinrich Mountain who directed fire for the land and sea batteries from "Eagle's Nest." By evening the Germans believed that they had the best of the day's struggle. They were correct.

Kamio ordered that the 1200 foot look-out post had to be reduced. A contingent of 300 men called "Kesshitai" (men resolved to die) was under command of a Captain Sato. In World War II the suicide pilots were called Kamikaze (Divine Wind). They reached the base of the rugged peak after nightfall on September 27. The night long ascent was slow and hazardous. The Germans had poured oil and soap on the rocks making it even more difficult to climb.

By early dawn the two opponents were engaged in battle. Sato was mortally wounded as was the second in command. For several hours the furious firefight continued. The fifty four Germans were able to maintain their defensive positions against six to one odds. The Japanese suffered substantial casualties and were unable to advance further.

Meanwhile, the Germans continued sending messages of their on-going battle as well as spotting artillery targets. Finally at noon a second party of Japanese appeared from the opposite side of the mountain. When the German officer offered to surrender the post in exchange for freedom to retreat under truce, the Japanese at first seemed to agree. But to his surprise and ignoring his white flag of truce, they seized him hostage. His men then threw some of their weapons and equipment over the cliff, released the remaining carrier pigeons and surrendered. A German sergeant and eleven men managed to escape and fought their way back to Tsingtau unscathed. Forty three others were taken prisoner. The Germans suffered only a few non-fatal casualties. The Japanese losses were 24 killed and over a hundred wounded. Their control of the peak was now the turning point of the siege.

To deprive the Germans any more communication with the outside world, Kamio sent part of his cavalry regiment to the town of Kiaochow a day's hard ride. They were to patrol the northern and western shore of the bay. Tsingtau would receive no more information, supplies or men by water, although carrier pigeons still flew in with messages for several weeks longer.

The German defenders now had no observation over the Japanese lines except the single aircraft and the "Yellow Sausage."

The captive balloon was sent up several times after the fall of the "Eagle's Nest" but was finally hit by Japanese artillery that put four shrapnel shells in the big gas bag. The observer, Lieutenant Hans Weihed was fortunate to be reeled in unhurt. He agreed heartily that the balloon, with seventy to eighty holes in it, not be used again, at least not with him.

A humerous, albeit conflicting, anecdotal story was reported to have occurred. The Germans devised a unique method to locate Japanese artillery positions. They sent up a large weather balloon with a small dummy in a laundry basket. Another report, probably more accurate, said that the second reconnaissance balloon was used. They had dressed a clothes manikin in a uniform, hung two pop bottles taped together around its neck as field glasses and included a broom handle for a weapon.

The decoy got loose from the cable. Whether intentionally or not was not reported. The Japanese could have assumed it was a balloon escaping the city with dispatches because they fired several dozen artillery rounds uselessly, but which did reveal some of their gun positions. Even the Allied ships failed to hit the balloon as it blew out into the Yellow sea toward Korea.

The military leaders of the day all used the same or similar textbooks, and they had all learned one basic lesson of warfare, everything else being equal, "It is the commander with the most complete knowledge of his enemy who wins the battle". The general term "intelligence" has been applied to this military knowledge. Every major power in the world has used paid espionage agents. But though this kind of information might well reveal the long-term strategic goals of an enemy, it will not reveal to a military commander in the field "what lies over the hill." This is the kind of immediate information that wins battles...the lack of it loses.

Plüschow's frail aeroplane was now the only method of aerial reconnaissance. The Japanese realized this fact and concentrated their efforts to shoot it down. When their artillery, firing shrapnel shells, failed to do so, the Japanese sent their planes after him. He often met enemy flyers in the air, but acting upon instructions, avoided combat with them. One day, however, when engrossed in his task of surveying the enemy's positions, he suddenly felt violent disturbances in the air which he believed to be air pockets from the mountains until he glanced up and saw a bi-wing land plane above him. Its observer dropped several bombs on him, all near misses. He swerved and dipped low. The German artillery observers, who had seen the enemy machine above him and saw Plüschow suddenly drop from their view, were most surprised when he returned safely and unharmed.

Some historians claim that the first air-to-air combat took place over Tsingtau on September 28, 1914. However, the French, previously secretive of their air operations learned of the Asian air battles and issued an official communique on November 8.

"Sept. 3rd—In the course of a reconnaissance (over Europe) a French pilot was attacked by a German aviator. The latter was promptly pursued by a second French aviator, who, subjecting him to a violent rifle fusillade, forced him precipitately to descend." No names or further particulars were given.

If true, and there is doubt, then the German-Japanese air-to-air duel must be clarified as "the first (over China) with pilots shooting at each other with pistols over Tsingtau on September 28." There is one report noted in Plüschow's diary that he "pursued his enemy colleague and shot him down."

He got the opportunity to climb above a Japanese machine and fired 30 rounds from a 9 millimeter Parabellum Mauser known as a "broom-handle" pistol. There was only one pilot in the Farman at the time and the plane spun out of control and crashed.

After enjoying the satisfaction of seeing his opponent destroyed, he was tempted to repeat the experience, but his orders to keep himself and his machine intact were too strict to allow him to risk another encounter or even discuss the matter. Plüschow didn't "officially" report the incident since he had disobeyed direct orders.

Perhaps that is why there was no official German report of the incident as it probably happened out of sight of Tsingtau deep over Japanese positions.

However, a Japanese aviator, Lieutenant Shigematsu flying a Maurice Farman, was listed as killed in action in 1914, the only one that year. No other particulars were noted.

Tsingtau was bombed regularly, by the nine Japanese Navy and Army planes, although rather ineffectively from the German point of view.

Extracts from the Japan Weekly Mail of October 21, 1914 stated;

"One of our monoplanes flew over the enemy's position, and brought to our Army headquarters extremely useful report."

"The seaplanes have been contributing more important service to our movement recently. On September 21st, Lieut. Wada and Sub-Lieut. Fujise made a flight over Tsing-tao and after spying out the general conditions of the enemy, threw down several bombs, two of which hit the base of the defence works on the southern end of an arsenal and seem to have destroyed it. During this reconnoitering, the seaplane was shot at from the enemy on land and sea and although several shots narrowly missed the machine, the aviators returned safely."

"On September 22nd, Lieut. Yamada and Sub-Lieut. Iikura on a seaplane reconnoitred again over Tsing-tao and dropped several bombs, one of which hit and exploded on the eastern corner of the barracks of the Bismarck forts. (Meyer-Waldeck's command center was in the basement bunker.) The seaplane received shots from the enemy, but escaped unhurt."

"On Sept 24th, Lieut. Wada and Sub-Lieut. Takebe on a seaplane, and Lieut. Yamada and Sub-Lieut. Osaki on another, scouted over Tsing-tao, and after having made important survey of the enemy's position, bombed the German destroyer, the forts, the barracks, the wireless station and the aerodrome, the effect of which is believed to have been good."

On September 27th Lieut.-Commander Kaneko, Lieut Wada and Lieut.-Engineer Hanajima on a seaplane, Sub-Lieut. Osaki and Fujise on another, and Sub Lieuts. Takebe and Itakura on still another, made effective reconnoitring over Tsing-tao and threw bombs on the wireless station and the aerodrome. They were shot at by the enemy, but none suffered the slightest damage."

Based on this description and the picture postcard photos made by Takahashi the spy, Japanese illustrators painted the scene of the planes over the city. These and dozens of other propaganda pictures were published in Japan during the siege, some of which are shown in this book.

In retaliation, the German arsenal produced some explosive devices for Plüschow to drop on the Japanese. These consisted of coffee canisters, the size of a Benzin petrol can filled with up to 25 sticks of dynamite, scrap iron and horse shoe nails. On the bottom, detonators were fashioned out of fulminate of mercury cartridge caps set off by a firing pin when struck.

Plüschow:
"I was a little afraid of these devices and handled them as one would a raw egg. I was always glad to get rid of them. Once I hit a torpedo boat, but the thing did not explode. A few times I almost hit a transport steamer. I was successful when I threw a bomb in the middle of a Japanese command center and dispatched thirty "Yellows" to Hades."

In order to reduce the weight, he would fly without his boots, sometimes without his flying jacket; even his "medicinal" flask of blackberry brandy. On shorter flights, he would also cut his fuel by one third. It was fortunate that Plüschow was less than five and a half feet and weighed only 135 pounds.

Plüschow only used these primitive explosives a few times, once when he located the British, who the Germans blamed for Japan's declaration of war. The devices were good only as anti-personnel bombs and he had to dive dangerously low to be accurate. He was still under orders to protect the plane at all costs.

Plüschow:

"I was very angry when I surveyed the camp of our enemies and located a different style tent. It was the British! I sent down our real Javanese stuff for their morning coffee. On the can filled with dynamite was written "Sietas, Plambeck & Co., best Java coffee." According to later English reports, the bomb hit the roof of their mess tent, but merely bounced back and did not explode. I soon stopped throwing bombs. The effect did not justify the trouble or danger to my plane."

By September 28, the German troops had pulled back along the entire front to the protection of the main line of defense by the redoubts and the "big ditch." The following description of events by Plüschow is anecdotal and somewhat philosophical.

"On September 28, we were locked behind the main barrier. At the same time an attack started from the sea. Early in the morning on this day, I sat contentedly in my bath tub before a long flight, when suddenly a deafening noise started. Because our artillery had been thundering for days and nights, I did not pay particular attention to this new sound, but only attributed it to the firing of our 28-centimeter howitzers of the Bismarck platoon which had been so far silent and conserving ammunition. My villa was directly beneath it a few hundred meters.

I sent my petty officer to my plane to check if everything was secure. But only after a few minutes he came running back breathlessly and pale and reported: "Flying officer, we have to leave the villa quickly. They are shooting at us from four large warships. One of the heavy grenades (explosive shells) just exploded by the hanger, but the plane is safe and nobody is hurt."

"I was out of the bath immediately almost forgetting to dress. Two minutes later I stood next to my plane which was in great danger from the explosions. Together my men and I moved the precious bird to another corner of the field where it was safe behind a slope. As I couldn't fly today until the craters were filled in, I ran to the coastal command post to watch the bombardment.

This command post was situated on a hill from which we had an ideal view of Tsingtau. From here the grenades, many 30.5-cm (12 inch explosive shells) could be seen as they hit. During the next weeks, whenever I was not flying, I sat up here in the fresh air watching the bombardment.

The explosions and the general noise was increased because of the echoing effect of the surrounding mountains. One after the other the 30.5-cm shells from the ships hit and we thought that Tsingtau would be turned into ruins. This was an incredible feeling, but we got used to it very quickly. One is so completely helpless when grenades hit and there is nothing else to do but to wait until it all may end. A bit of luck is necessary of course in order not to stand where one of those devilish things fall.

The enemy ships stood far out to sea so that our artillery could not reach them. They were in complete safety! Thank God the damage that the shelling caused wasn't great, and that many of the shells were duds. It was like watching an exercise in bad target practice.

On the evening of the same day, I witnessed a sorrowful occurrence. Our gunboats *Cormorant, Iltis,* and *Luchs* were sunk by us after they had given up their armament. (Transferred to land defenses) This was a sad sight indeed. The three ships, tied one behind the other, were pulled by a steamer into deep water. It looked as if these ships, once alive, knew they were being dragged to the slaughterhouse. In the bay the ships were ignited. They blew up, burned and sank."

General Kamio held his men back to dig in and wait for the siege guns to be in place. He had decided on a siege against the German defenses instead of an all out assault. This was exactly the opposite of what Meyer-Waldeck assumed he would do.

Plüschow:
"The operation of the Japanese army was a great puzzle to us. After the first major attack, we all thought that the enemy would now try to storm the stronghold immediately. But nothing happened. We simply didn't understand the enemy who must know how weak we were. They only had to cross the mine field, and over the big ditch and wire entanglements to be inside.

Then wild rumors began to circulate.

"The Japanese do not dare to attack. The situation in Europe looks too good for us!

And then: "The Americans will send their navy to rescue us! The Japanese will have to withdraw!"

Another: "The Japanese want to starve us to death. They want to get Tsingtau as undamaged as possible!"

But all this was speculation. Slowly and systematically, and without our being able to stop them, the Japanese landed their troops, constructed roads and railroads. They brought in the heaviest siege artillery and ammunition. They dug in right in front of our defense obstacles and slowly worked forward towards our lines.

Now my most important job was the reconnaissance of the heavy enemy artillery positions. Day after day, weather and propellers permitting, I was at my plane at dawn. Usually I took off heading south. At the end of the field, approximately where Fort Hweichuen Point meets the sea, strong air pockets formed. The plane would seem to drop down right from under me. I pulled it up again just clearing the artillery of the fort. They would see me climbing and would hold their fire. Then the plane would drop once more, and often I levelled out only inches above the surface of the sea. The artillerymen at the fort had a small boat ready to rescue me in case of a crash.

I would then gain altitude and circle to the west past Arkona island, south of Tsingtau, over the power plant, harbor and docks, then head north. When the altimeter reached 2000 meters, I thanked God; and tried to reach the enemy lines on the shortest way possible to begin my observations."

The Rumpler-Taube was called by the French "The Invisible Aeroplane." This was the world's first "stealth" aircraft. The fabric which covered the fuselage and wings seemed translucent when the craft was approaching 350 meters (1000 feet). On a really bright day it was invisible at 1200 meters (3937 feet). Plüschow was aware of these unique characteristics of his aircraft, but he flew even higher to be sure he was unseen because so many days were cloudy and overcast and the sound of the motor could be heard.

Plüschow:
"As soon as I was over the enemy, I slowed down the engine so that the plane stayed at the same altitude by itself. The speed was only 80 kilometers an hour. (50 mph) Then I took out the map, held it against the steering wheel, took pencil and paper and began to look for the enemy. I let go of the wheel and controlled the plane with my feet.

I would circle around one position until I had surveyed everything, entered it on the map and made exact notes and sketches. I soon had considerable practice so that I could watch and write for up to two hours. When my body became stiff, I changed my position and observed out the opposite side. It was not easy to see down because the wings were only separated from the fuselage by about 30 centimeters (1 ft) and the wings extended 76 centimeters past the rear of the cockpit. To get a good view I had to turn to look back as well as looking for enemy aircraft. When I had observed enough or the tank gage or clock reminded me that it was time to land, I would return by the same flight pattern, circling the dockyard and the city and coming in from the sea.

When I reached the landing strip, I stopped the engine and glided down in circles. Four minutes later I was safely on the ground. The speed was necessary. While the Japanese might not see me when up high, a plane at my same altitude could easily let the ground positions know I was coming in. I once saw a white cloth flutter down from the giant birds signalling I was about to land.

That lovely morning, I noticed lots of small grey-white cloud puffs 300 meters over the landing site. They looked beautiful from above. I soon realized that the Japanese were firing 105 mm shrapnel. But what could I do? My benzin gage showed nearly empty. From 2000 meters I nose-dived my plane and four minutes later landed safely. Immediately I steered it into the hanger protected underground with my crew helping me.

Now it was my turn to use a ruse. Sometimes when I was still over enemy positions, I switched off the engine and veered vertically down towards a corner of my landing site so that the Japanese thought I had been hit. They were so surprised that their shrapnel shell fire only reached the landing field after I was safe."

Besides the regular three overweight men who restrained the aircraft until it got up to speed for takeoffs, the plane needed a device to brake it when he came in steep and fast for a landing. The field was being pocked-marked with shell holes that were continually being filled by coolie gangs. Plüschow's plane didn't have the newer Rumpler-Taube claw braking device which was operated from the cockpit and would dig into the ground when applied. But Plüschow devised a landing arresting gear that was primitive compared to those used aboard today's aircraft carriers. But it was effective.

Between two bamboo poles a line was strung on the ground so that when his plane landed, the ground crew could lift the rope to catch the skid at the tail of the aircraft. Two sets of coal sacks, the first partially filled with sand and the second slightly heavier were tied to both ends of the rope and would be dragged along slowing and then stopping the aircraft.

One of the concerns for Kamio was that the Japanese could not always distinguish between European friends and foes. Japanese infantrymen had mistreated some British officers, shot at others and wounded an enlisted man in the chest. Lance Corporal Thomas was the first British casualty, albeit from "friendly" fire. Both Allies agreed that the British would wear a white patch on their helmets and a red armband except that now it made a better target for the Germans.

A German contingent attempted to fool the Japanese by discarding their regular headgear and wearing the small off-duty caps that looked similiar to the Japanese. However the idea backfired when they were mistaken for the enemy and shot at. No German was injured.

Another concern for Kamio was the lack of effective Anglo-Japanese naval participation. Admiral Kato was not eager to come within range of the accurate gunners at the big forts, especially Hweichuen Point. Besides he was wary of the mine fields. There was a good reason.

On September 30 the hydro-plane carrier, *Wakamiya Maru* hit a mine blowing a gaping six meter hole in her engine room. The crew barely managed to beach the vessel on Tschu Tsch-tao island. No aircraft were damaged, because two days previously three of the planes had left the ship for a base established at Lao Shan harbor. The Japanese merely unloaded the last plane from below decks and lowered it into the sea where it flew off to the navy sea-plane installation. Their base was to eventually become similar to the Army's Air Corp at Tsimo.

The latter was an old factory building which housed the workshops and dining and eating facilities. Living quarters were decorated with shoji screens, tatami matted flooring and an authentic Japanese bath house. Korean "comfort women" were also employed. There was also a rock garden, a pond for Koi and goldfish, imported Bonsai trees, plants and stone lanterns. Military aviators, apparently even then, were the elite!

An hour after the last hydro-plane left, an auxiliary tender coming to help the mother-ship, hit another mine and sank, losing several men. Then another small auxiliary vessel struck a mine the very next day and also went down with four men.

Further humiliating the Japanese, Plüschow flew over the unarmed repair ship *Kwanto Maru*, and dropped two bombs. Both exploded when they hit the water inches from the hull and sounded like an enormous temple gong being struck. No damage was done.

The Germans had sown a mere 296 mines, but the Japanese now suspected far more and gave the waters around the mouth of the bay due respect, even though their mine sweepers had only discovered two mines. A later Japanese report claimed the Germans had laid over one thousand mines, another rumor said that it was four thousand. These false reports were apparently made to "save face."

One day when Plüschow was sketching the positions of the Japanese seaplane hangers on his chart, he saw a huge double decker emerge and take off from the bay. He went on with his survey as he

112

thought he would have plenty of time before it could reach his altitude, about 2000 meters and actually see him. Thirty minutes later he paused to take stock of the situation and was amazed to see the enemy rapidly approaching. Plüschow remembered the lesson of the hawk and the dove. He decided to climb higher, but after a short time he made the unpleasant discovery that he had reached the top of his ceiling a little under 3000 meters (9843 feet). Meanwhile the Japanese continued to ascend after him. It dawned on Plüschow that the enemy had laid a trap to cut him off from his base. He promptly turned and fled.

To his delight he found that, although inferior in climbing power, because of his improvised propeller, his Taube was faster and more maneuverable. He reached Tsingtau well ahead of his pursuer and did a steep nose-dive for the airfield, plunging through the usual cotton puffs of shrapnel before landing safely.

It was the take-offs and landings from Iltis Platz that were dangerous. The Japanese would concentrate their artillery fire on the tiny field as soon as they saw him lift off or approach to land. But throughout the siege the Taube was only punctured a few times by shrapnel and never badly damaged. The shell holes in the field were constantly filled by Chinese coolies supervised by the ground crew. Once they found an unexploded bomb made from a 77 mm shell. Plüschow taped his calling card on it and wrote; "Not nice to drop such hard things on a fellow aviator. I give it back." Next day he dropped it on the Japanese seaplane sheds. It still didn't explode, so they must have gotten the message. Plüschow failed to mention this episode in his daily report.

The Japanese Navy, angered at the lone "sky-spy" bombing their ships and air base and eluding their planes and artillery continued to bomb the decoy at the old hanger. Several times they destroyed the fake Taube, but Plüschow was up and flying the very next day. It must have perplexed the Japanese, knowing there had originally been only two aircraft as reported by their spies, one of which was totally demolished in a crash. They must have wondered how the bombed plane could be repaired so quickly each day. The ground crew also had the task of rebuilding the decoy and moving it about the field away from the actual hanger which never did come under fire.

The Navy planes made a total of 49 sorties, dropping 199 bombs, listing 8 hits and 16 probables. How many of these were wasted on the Taube decoy was never reported.

# CHAPTER 9

## TYPHOON "DAH-FUNG" (Big Wind)

The Japanese had collected substantial information about Tsingtau's main defenses, the city, the harbor and the environs of the protectorate thanks to Takahashi and other informers. Their maps were excellent. It was the inner redoubts, machine-gun nests and artillery positions Kamio was uncertain about. His army intelligence continued compiling more details on the German defense line. Japanese aircraft were now flying photo reconnaissance at 1300 meters where they felt reasonably safe from German fire, but this was also too high to be of much good. The German decoys and camouflage were excellent.

The Japanese plan was to wait for all the large siege guns to be in position. The score of pontoon barges used to carry them ashore from the transport ships were continously coming and going. Two floating cranes at the pontoon pier off-loaded the 15 ton cannon and placed them on the rail cars. They were transported steadily but slowly over the narrow gage railway which now extended from Laoshan bay to Litsun only ten kilometers from the German lines.

Major General Kishino Watanabe was assigned the command of the land-siege guns. There were more than 140 cannon and howitzers. The sizes ranged from 120 mm to 280 mm and included 100 mm and 150 mm naval guns. Cement platforms were constructed for the "ginger-beer bottles" as the British called the 11 inch howitzers. The work was done mostly by Chinese laborers.

Kamio's transportation supply-lines continued to use the

hundreds of efficient two-man wheelbarrows. Their owners were forced to draw them. Each large single-wheeled vehicle could carry up to 350 pounds of supplies even over bad roads. From the air they looked like ants moving both ways in double file.

The Japanese had also commandeered even more two-wheel pony carts from the Chinese making the total about 800. There was plenty of Chinese coolie power; an estimated 10,000 men. When the shooting began most of the Chinese working for the Germans in Tsingtau had fled, and were forced to work for new taskmasters.

Plüschow:

"My Chinese cook Moritz left me when the first shot hit, and one evening soon after, all the other Chinese servants, disappeared without notice. After a few days, a new Chinese cook arrived, called Wilhelm, who told me with big gestures: "You, "Dragon Master". I good cook. I not run away as no-good others. I not afraid. I make plenty good chau-chau." I believed him and promised five dollars extra. All went quite well until one day the first enemy shells exploded near my house, and Mr. Wilhelm disappeared just as his predecessors had."

It was suspicious that the last Chinese cook showed up so soon after the other servants left, even as the shelling and bombing was still continuing and he only stayed a short time. Japanese army intelligence, were known to have used Chinese spies and Korean officers, who looked Chinese, to infiltrate the city. Never-the-less Plüschow never commented on it, only that the aerial bombing of the airfield let up, replaced by howitzer shells which created large craters that were constantly being filled at night. It made it very difficult to take off and land.

For the Chinese fleeing the city, it was "from the frying pan into the fire." As stated before, more than ten thousand coolies were impressed into service as practically slave labor to work for food and Japanese military money, the latter being useless. Most of the "grunt" labor, moving heavy equipment, building the molds and pouring concrete for gun platforms were done by the coolies under Japanese direction.

The laborers were housed in Japanese army tents within barbed-wire compounds, "for their protection" as it was explained to them. This was the very thing that Meyer-Waldeck had decided against. The Japanese were inclined to billet their own soldiers in the numerous Chinese villages. Most of the inhabitants who could, fled. Whether the Chinese gave information to the Germans or not is doubtful; but the occupied villages were almost invariably subjected to heavy shell fire after Plüschow reported the evidence of Japanese troops in several villages.

On October 2 the Japanese prepared a document proposing to the Germans, a four hour truce, to allow the non-combatants in Tsingtau to be evacuated, and the dead to be retrieved and buried. It was signed by Vice Admiral Kato and Lt. General Kamio who sent a complimentary duplicate to acting Brigadier General Barnardiston. The Brigadier immediately insisted that, as an ally, his signature also be added to the paper. Kamio was visibly shocked at the request, but did accept Barnardiston's proposal that they both contact their respective governments.

The truce was delayed until a clarification of the dispute arrived from the British War Office in London. They quoted earlier instructions to Barnardiston: "You will be subject to the control of the Japanese Commander and will cooperate with as a complete formation... etc." The reply moved slowly through British chains of command.

Finally on October 12, a short note arrived from the British Embassy in Tokyo stating that Barnardiston should be a signatory to any declaration, only when Kamio desired it. The Japanese commander did not desire it. Instead he changed his own title to "Commander in Chief of the Army Besieging Tsingtao." The human relations in the field between Japanese and British were now even more strained.

This is the direct English translation of the formally prepared controversial draft from the Japanese archives:

Headquarters of the Army Besieging Tsingtao, October, 1914

Your Excellency;

*"At this moment when you are heroically defending the fortress of Tsingtao, the undersigned have the honour to inform you of the most benevolent and gracious wish of His Majesty the Emperor of Japan. The Imperial Intention is to spare the lives of those non-belligerents of the Belligerent powers and people of Neutral Countries now at Tsingtao who may desire to avert the loss and injury which they might sustain as the result of our siege operations.*

*In case you have a desire to concur to this Imperial Wish, more detailed informations shall be forwarded."*
Lieutenant-General Mitsuomi Kamio,
Commander in Chief of the Army Besieging Tsingtao.
Vice-Admiral Sadakichi Kato,
Commander in Chief of the Fleet Blockading Tsingtao.
To: Captain Meyer Waldeck

The Governor welcomed this opportunity. He sent his adjutant, Major Georg von Kayser to discuss the particulars of the proposed truce. The Major, wearing all his medals, including a Japanese order, led a mounted party that included a translator, a trumpeter, a horse-holder and a white flag carrier.

He was met in the village of Tungwu-tschia Tsun by a Japanese Colonel, Isomura and entourage astride their immaculately groomed horses. He too was wearing his medals also including a

German one. The tall Germans sitting astride their Mongolian ponys with battle stained coats were in sharp contrast to the Japanese. They saluted, shook hands, and read and translated the Japanese proposal. They briefly discussed the siege; the Japanese Colonel indicating his sorrow over the war. A Captain Yamada asked von Kayser to give his best regards to his friend Captain Walther Stecher. Then they shook hands, saluted and rode off.

Meyer-Waldeck immediately issued a public announcement of the chance to evacuate non-combatants. Among the Germans only two women nurses requested to leave. The other German women and children elected to stay in the city. Willys Peck, the American Consul also wanted to depart, as ordered by Washington, along with two very happy Chinese servants. An American newspaperman A.M. Brace remained in Tsingtau. The Germans refused exit to another man, Edgar Kopp. They believed that he and eleven Hindu Indians possessed too much military information.

The evacuees departed on the small steamer *Tsimo*. The trip took them 30 kilometers across Kiaochow Bay to the fishing village of Tapu-tau which was the present sea terminal for the town of Kiaochow. Some fifty years previously the bay had been washing the breakwater of Kiaochow, but since has silted in.

The Japanese were on hand to closely supervise the unloading of the baggage which was searched for official German documents, of which there were none. The III SeeBatalion Marine band was aboard ship and played several German songs as the evacuees landed. Then as the vessel moved away from the dock, everyone on board and ashore waved handkerchiefs and hats. Peck "found the ceremonies highly moving and unusual in the middle of a war," as was reported by him to the Secretary of State in Washington.

Some Chinese reports advanced the opinion that the truce was only offered so the Japanese could gather and bury their dead which was quite considerable. The Japanese did bury several German soldiers complete with full military honors and flowers. The Chinese

119

witnesses said that a man was on hand taking photographs, no doubt for propaganda purposes.

During the truce a Japanese officer walked out on the glacis and challenged any German to duel with swords. In true Bushido tradition the cavalry officer grasped his samurai sword and wildly twirled the blade about his head and body. The short stocky warrior emphasized each exaggerated thrust and prancing foot movement with loud shouts and grunts. His men stood back at a distance from their strutting officer. They all waved tiny Japanese paper flags attached to chopsticks and cheered him on with shouts of "Banzai." Rifles were slung over their backs in a nonthreatening position.

A tall blonde German officer with dueling scars on his face stepped forward. Having been brought up on swordplay he was a champion duelist familiar with both saber and fencing foil. Having only observed the flamboyant Oriental swordplay, he had never fought such an adversary. It was West pitted against East.

The German calmly removed his jacket and drew his steel. Gripping the sword firmly in his right hand he stepped forward, stopped and at attention raised the saber to his face in a salute. The Japanese swordsman brought his booted legs together like two parenthesis and bowed slightly. Immediately he assumed the wild sword swinging mode and attacked.

The German parried easily with the disciplined one-arm European dueling stance; one leg forward; one arm back; sword extended. As both sides looked on, he soon dispatched the challenger, who died still believing that a Samurai could beat a European swordsman.

The Japanese knew that shooting the winner in retaliation would break the truce and their honor. They contained their anger and chagrin and hurridly retrieved the body while the German officer turned his back and sauntered proudly back to his men.

According to the agreement, no aerial flights were permitted during the 4 hour cease-fire truce between 12:20 and 4:40 p.m., when the evacuation vessel returned to port. Then the war resumed.

One German eyewitness wrote; "It was interesting to see at the start of the truce, the Japanese crawling out of their holes from all sides, waving their little flags with red dots. Then when the truce time had elapsed, they disappeared from view just as quickly."

Just before sunset, Plüschow took off for a quick aerial survey and noticed several farm fields that had apparently been used as burial sites.

Kamio pressured Admiral Kato into a major bombardment on October 14. The Japanese flagship *Suwo* and others were listed to increase their range and commenced firing at a distance of 15,750 meters. The target, Hweichuen fort replied immediately, but her shells fell 900 meters short. The Germans then aimed for *Tango* which was nearer and firing at Iltis fort. Suddenly the heavy cruiser was surrounded by fountains of water. She immediately withdrew.

As described briefly before, the British battleship *Triumph* was last in line just east of Iltis Huk thinking that the point of land would protect it from Hweichuen fort. The gun crews fired some thirty shells at Iltis fort from a fixed position.

Shortly after 10 o'clock when the ship was preparing to depart, lookouts saw a puff of smoke on Huichuen fort and a few seconds later a 240 mm explosive shell hit just below the mainmast, killing only one sailor, but wounding two others while causing substantial damage. As the *Triumph* hurriedly steamed seaward, a second shell tossed a huge column of water into the air at it's former position. The ship was put out of commission for several weeks while undergoing repairs at sea by the Japanese. Admiral Kato would now wait until there was a massive land bombardment and offensive before endangering his ships again.

On October 15 a tremendous rain storm, the tail of a Typhoon, came to the aid of the besieged Germans. For two days some 38 centimeters (15 inches) of water fell. Hostilities and investment activities came to a halt. Flash floods poured down the mountain gullies and ravines. A major Japanese supply and ammunition depot was swept away by Litsun creek, transformed into a raging river. Everything washed into the bay. When the German warships saw the floating crates and boxes, they believed them to be floating Japanese mines and tried to detonate them with gun fire. There were angry outcries and finger pointing by the sailors when it was learned that several of the objects were beer barrels.

At Liu-ting a 3 meter high wave of flood water devastated another supply base. It poured down from the mountains like from a ruptured dam. At Tsimo another 10 foot high flash flood caused havoc with the Japanese supplies. The Army airbase was turned into a landing field suitable for only seaplanes. Before the storm hit the Navy had dragged their bi-planes high and dry on the soft sand using log rollers and bamboo mats under the pontoons. The narrow gage railway system was eroded in numerous places and several sections washed away. Troops stumbled around in the water and mud trying to retrieve their belongings, military supplies and weapons and bailing out their trenches waist deep of water. The Germans on relatively higher ground were also flooded. Nothing was dry, clothing or bedding. The shell craters in Plüschow's air field became ponds and small lakes. Ditches were dug to try and drain them to little avail.

The pontoon landing-wharf in Laoshan bay was washed away by the high seas. A hundred sampans, used as landing barges, were wrecked and 24 soldiers drowned. The Chinese casualties or dead were usually never tallied, peace or war.

The Chinese population had been hurt especially badly for the second time in as many months. Their stone and wood houses, held together with mud, had, for the most part collapsed and many were carried away by the wild surging rivers. Numerous Chinese died in the floods. Many had been robbed of all their possessions.

The ones who lived in villages inside the German lines now wandered through the streets as homeless beggars. Many of the Chinese knew a few words of Pidgin German. It was hard to turn a hungry person away who tried to beg in your own tongue. The German troops shared their bread and food with them as far as humanly possible.

The silence of the Japanese land guns and the interminable waiting for the "second boot to drop" began to unnerve the Germans. To offset this depression, the torpedo-boat *S-90* was ordered on a search and destroy mission.

Plüschow:

"Late in the evening of October 17, a group of officers and I stood anxiously on the coastal command post. The old torpedo-boat S-90, commanded by Lieutenant Brunner was supposed to leave port. She was going to do her last and hardest job; to breakthrough the blockade of enemy torpedo-boat destroyers and to attack one of the enemy ships. It was a clear night; the moon set around 10 o'clock. Then at 11 we saw a long grey shadow which moved slowly through the water close to the Pearl Mountains to the south heading out of the bay.

The boat disappeared in the blackness. We watched anxiously and expected every moment that the searchlights would flare up and enemy shelling begin. But all remained quiet. It was midnight, then 12:30 and we began to relax. The enemy had not seen our ship. She must now be close to the main body of the Japanese fleet. Minutes seemed like hours. Nobody spoke.

Then suddenly at one o'clock, a huge fire column was seen; then the searchlights pierced the sky. We could faintly hear the gun fire. At 1:30, we received the following wireless message;

"Have attacked enemy cruiser with three torpedoes, all of them hit. Cruiser exploded. Being chased by enemy destroyer. Return to Tsingtau is cut. Try to escape south. Will explode boat if necessary. Signed: Brunner."

The search and destroy mission of the *S-90* was successful to a point. The torpedo-boat approached to within 500 yards of a Japanese vessel unnoticed and fired two torpedoes. Then at 300 yards fired a third. The last torpedo found its target. The cruiser *Takaschio* was carrying 120 mines which exploded simultaneously. A huge fire ball shot into the night sky. Of the Japanese crew 253 perished. (Ten men of the ship's full complement had previously left the vessel). Only three men were saved. The Japanese reported officially that the ship had struck a mine. This was published in the Allied and American press. (The true details were revealed by the Germans and later by Plüschow.)

(Author's note): One report was that two torpedoes hit the ship but the same above description was published in the Journal of the U.S. Artillery.

The terrific explosion had the same concussion effect on the *S-90* as a depth charge on a submarine; it started her plates. Leaking badly, Brunner decided not to attempt returning to port. Instead he headed south for 110 kilometers (60 miles) and was able to beach the vessel on Chinese soil. The ship was then blown up with her last torpedo. The crew eventually made their way to Nanking and were interned.

More important to the Japanese, than the embarrassment over the ship disaster, was that the *S-90* was on the loose. Their only available aircraft were being overhauled from the effects of the Typhoon. The army airfield was still a sea of mud. Land observers filed conflicting reports of the torpedo-boat's whereabouts. Until the ship could be found, Admiral Kato suspended all supply shipments and sent the fleet dashing around searching for the *S-90* not unlike a great "feeding frenzy" of sharks.

The local Chinese government officials claimed the vessel and raised a Chinese flag on the mast. The Japanese discovered the wreck a few days later on October 20 with one of their seaplanes. A landing party from a surface ship boarded her and replaced the flag with their own "rising sun" ensign. This friction between the two Asian nations was widely reported in the European and American press. Not long after the Japanese removed their flag but still assigned a gunboat to guard the prize.

The Japanese navy also reported that they had made a great find; "charts left behind by the crew that indicated the location of the German mine fields."

A foot-note of the historian Charles B. Burdick concerning the above incident states;

"Brunner's costly error is difficult to understand, since he was a careful man in all details. When he destroyed his ship, he insisted upon the most thorough job possible."

(AUTHOR'S NOTE): Since the crew were not pursued at the time of beaching the vessel and in no immediate hurry to leave the ship, could it not have been possible that a chart with false mine positions was "planted" by the Germans? Even with this supposedly great "treasure chart" the Japanese claimed to have found, they continued to lose ships to German mines during the siege and even weeks after Tsingtau surrendered. The exact number will be listed later.

Then there is another more likely possibility.

The Chinese fishermen or farmers who first found the S-90 in all probability looted the vessel and were not likely to have left the German charts behind.

FOOT-NOTE:

The author, while living in Tsingtao in 1939, visited a large five-masted north China trading junk over 200 years old and was shown an old German navigational chart. The Chinese Captain asked Whittaker, who owned his own sailing yacht, for the translation of several German words and navigational terms. The author, with some knowledge of German, was well versed in Chinese besides being a proficient navigator. In hindsight, had he traded his British Admiralty chart for the old German one as the Chinese ship-master suggested, he would have had a historic document possibly refuting the Japanese claim.

Not knowing the complete details of the Tsingtau Siege at the time, the significance of the many curious position circles with cross-bearing lines drawn on the badly-worn chart was not apparent until the author began researching documents for this book 52 years later!

# CHAPTER 10

## MASSIVE BOMBARDMENT

On October 21, the status of the siege was as follows: The Germans had retired within the shelter of the line of redoubts, trenches and the "big ditch" of wire entanglements and mine fields. They were confining their efforts to heavy, but distant shell fire at specific targets that Plüschow could determine. The Japanese outposts and entrenchments had pushed forward completely across the peninsula from sea to bay, 1800 meters (one mile) from the German line, with some units dug in even closer. The many ravines and gullies made excellent protection for the Japanese who would inexorably dig their trenches toward the German line. They kept well hidden from German observation and gunfire. It was what the Germans called the "empty battlefield advance."

On October 23 a dozen foreign military observers arrived in Lao Shan bay by permission of the Imperial Government. The Japanese reception committee bowed and hissed and treated them with the utmost respect, but didn't help to expedite the visitors' investigations of the battlefield. The American Army Colonel, J.A. Irons, said caustically, in his writings;

"From personal experience, it is thought that military observers are nearly as much of a nuisance as newspaper correspondents." That was one of the more polite comments. Another of the observers wrote sarcastically;

"Nothing was lacking that tended to hamper our movements."

They were not allowed to visit troops, take photographs, or even observe the front. The Japanese were as secretive with their own Allies and neutrals as they were with their enemy.

On the other hand the 25 Japanese newspapermen, photographers and war artists, had much freer entre. The latter painted the dozen or so illustrated posters that were printed and circulated in Japan even while the siege was under way. The artist was helped by the numerous photographs taken over the years by the Tsingtau photographer Takahashi. As he was not mentioned in any of the reports, it can be assumed that Takahashi was still working undercover for Japanese intelligence.

Plüschow the "Sky Spy" could not be put out of action. The "One-Man German Air Force" could still fly missions high enough to be safe with his "stealth" plane. But it was difficult however, for him to accurately locate the Japanese because of the weather ravaged scars in the terrain, excellent camouflage of the enemy, decoys and constantly changing positions. The flyer noted the "empty battlefield" technique of the enemy. The Japanese had mounted many of their Naval cannon on rail cars that could be moved from place to place confusing the defenders.

Every effort was made by the Germans to facilitate Plüschow's aerial reconnaissance. Some 40 private cars and two dozen trucks in the city had been commandeered by the military. Vehicles were at a premium. Plüschow was privileged to have been given an automobile and a driver to be carried to and from his airplane. Upon his return each mission, he was immediately transported to the Bismarck bunker to personally report to the Commander-in-Chief and General Staff awaiting anxiously.

He was treated with the deference of an officer with a much higher rank than just a Flying Lieutenant. There was one report that he was given a field promotion to Oberleutnant but Plüschow's diary made no note of it. Since he was very publicity minded and kept a detailed diary he certainly would not have forgotten a promotion. A

128

photograph does show two full stripes of that rank on his uniform with decorations so this in all probability was taken later in Germany.

The Japanese Army and Navy Air Corps added something innovative to their operations — the first night bombing in history. There was a beautiful full moon on October 28, and a clear sky enough to distinguish targets from the air.

Four aircraft, two from each corps, loosed a number of bombs that observers said looked like "droppings" from giant birds in the night sky. The bombs screaming down from the heavens brought terror to the Chinese who could only hide in the cellars of their houses and were not fortunate to have a meter of ferro-cement over their heads like the Germans.

The Japanese Navy concentrated on the Iltis Platz and the harbor in retaliation to Plüschow's attempted bombing of their sea-plane tender and other vessels. The bombs did little except dig up the field and again damaged the canvas decoy plane. But it did keep the German flyer awake and envious of what he considered "large" bi-planes droning overhead with their load of bombs and a three man crew. As usual, the attempts to shoot them down with shrapnel only made it dangerous for the troops and the inhabitants of Tsingtau who ventured out into the open.

Only one of the Japanese Maurice Farman Navy seaplanes carried three men; A pilot, an officer-in-charge, who was also the observer and a "bomb thrower." The large open cockpit in the forward end of the 2.9 meter long fuselage had only one seat for the pilot. Behind him there was a box admidships running the length that doubled for seats for the other two men, and also contained the "bombs". These were actually 77 mm artillery shells from the Type 38 field gun. This 6.5 kilogram shell (14 lbs) was fitted with four stabilizing fins at the rear. Ten of these missiles could be carried, approximately the weight of one man. The plane could fly at the maximum of 96 km/hr (60 mph) for four and a half hours; less when they had a full load. The climb rate was 25 minutes to 1,000 meters or

131 feet per minute. The service ceiling was 3,000 meters (9842 feet). This Navy lead plane also had a two-way wireless and at times a machine-gun.

The Japanese tried heavier bombs made from 105 mm shells like those used in the Type 38 heavy field gun. The 16 kilogram missile was two and half times as heavy as the 77 mm bombs and too ungainly to be tossed by hand like the others. They were attached to the side of the fuselage and released by hand.

The other Navy and Army M-Farmans only carried two men each and were slightly slower, but their climb rate was faster.

The Japanese had by now considerable experience in bombing techniques, albeit primitive by today's standards. During bombing missions in the 3 passenger seaplane the observer and bomb thrower would have to squat or stand so the bombs could be accessible. If they had safety belts or harnesses, they were not shown in the propaganda illustrations of the planes flying over Tsingtau.

The plane would dive to 300 meters, and just as they would pull out of the dive at below a thousand feet, the bomber would throw or release the missile. Since both land and sea planes had no pontoons or wheel frames directly below the cockpit, it was tricky, but not too difficult to throw the shell directly down at the target. The accuracy still was a lot to be desired especially when several bombs were thrown in rapid sequence.

As stated in one Japanese report: "The planes also engaged in mine survey. They sunk the German mine-layer with make-shift aerial bombs made from ordinary gun shells."

There is a discrepancy in this report. There was no mention of this from the Germans or the American newspaperman Brace.

The Japanese report continued:

"As the German ack-ack guns were effective up to 2,000 meters (6562 feet), the Farman three-seater used to fly at 3,000 meters (9842 feet)."

Signal Hill was bombed several times both day and night,

along with the harbor area, the power plant, and Bismarck barracks. But there was only minor damage from the inaccurate bomb "throwing" and few casualties. There was an account of a bomb hitting a pigsty in Chinatown. "The pork meat was strewn about free for the taking. Also killed was the farmer."

Ever since the water pumping station at Litsun a month ago had been damaged by Japanese artillery and later captured, the secondary pumping station at Haipo creek was not large enough to provide full service. Water was rationed for only a few hours each day. Baths had become a rare luxury. Plüschow had access to a well near his house. Several times a day his coolie boy would carry 2 five gallon cans of water suspended on a bamboo shoulder pole. Plüschow never mastered the technique of the bobbing gait that distributed much of the weight to the springy pole.

The barracks, where Meyer-Waldeck had his bunker deep below in the "Ink Pot," had been evacuated by the regular troops on rotation from the front. They were now billeted in the houses of the Chinese who agreed to take them in for a price. Some of them were still occupied and the more affluent homes had a stock of food, gramophones to play, billiard tables and the amenities of normal living. The Chinese were very hospitable, thinking that with the German presence they would be better protected. They were also interested in guarding their belongings. Other men set up lodging in the vacated villas of the "ladies of the night." A number of the single men were quite familiar with the houses.

The men had to assemble for duty at 4:45 o'clock every morning on Deutschland street. The enterprising Chinese street hawkers would sell warm "Balinna," as the Chinese pronounced it, for breakfast. These were "Berliner Pfannkuchen (Jelly donuts) almost like from the Fatherland."

After eating and storing the donuts in their field pouches and filling their canteens with hot coffee, the sergeant would count the men off and thoroughly inspect everyone. They were each required to have 200 rifle cartridges in their pouches. Then they would march off to relieve the other men in the redoubts.

Chinese spies sent news by carrier pigeon that on October 28, half of the Thirty-sixth Sikh Battalion finally arrived (450 men) to relieve a company of Borderers. They usually were an impressive sight, tall, full-bearded and turbanned. The Indians were now unkempt and tired from their muddy overland march as well as recovering from the seasickness of a rough voyage and landing. They struggled over roads that were still unfit for travel with carts pulled by balky mules. The animals brought from Tientsin were unused to the improvised harnesses. They only covered nine kilometers in an eleven-hour march. The next day they made better time and after a brief rest and a visit from the Japanese Commanding General, the Sikhs reached a front-line position on October 30. They were of great interest to the short Japanese and even to the British who had not been stationed in India. That night when the Sikhs arrived at the British encampment they were shelled by the Germans. This made the British and the Japanese very suspicious of them. But it was actually Plüschow who had reported the new contingent of soldiers wearing different uniforms, turbans and fully bearded.

Plüschow:
"The Japanese came closer and closer; they had more and more heavy artillery in position. Several times a large Japanese infantry troop tried to storm us, but were defeated. Our soldiers were constantly under artillery fire. Our guns, too, were hardly ever quiet. Unfortunately, we were forced to use the little ammunition we had very frugally and only at known targets.

The extraordinary length of the siege, the constant artillery fire and the terrible tension finally took it's toll. My nerves began to crack. I could hardly eat. I rarely slept, and then only briefly. When I closed my eyes I had the maps in front of my eyes and saw the protectorate under me, destroyed by enemy guns. I heard the words of my commander-in-chief;

"Plüschow! remember that you are more important for the defense of Tsingtau than even our daily bread. Come back and keep the airplane safe. Remember how few grenades we have and that we use them based only on your observations. Remember your responsibilities."

"God knows that I remembered. I thought of nothing else but locating enemy positions, and I crossed them again and again in my mind wondering whether I had reported everything. Sometimes I fell asleep early in the morning totally exhausted. And as soon as I was asleep, my mechanic came to wake me up for the next mission."

It was imperative that the Germans learn about the status of Japanese readiness to start the main land offensive. On October 30, long before sunrise, but while it was getting light Plüschow took off at 4 a.m. There was no wind. The calm ocean looked like a grey silk quilt undulating as if stirred by the sea creatures it covered.

The three stalwart men restrained the Taube until it revved up to speed and the Dove was released into the air. He again flew far around Kiaochow Bay to gain altitude before he reached the Anglo-Japanese lines.

Plüschow:

"Once I had taken off and reached an altitude of some 100 meters, everything was all right again. But one thing depressed me terribly; I was always alone in my plane. If only I had a friend with me it would have been easier to keep a lookout for Japanese planes as I made notes. I always avoided birds, especially the white sea-birds in case they might be one of our message-carrying Tauben, and also because my propeller could again easily be broken.

133

When I could not fly for several days, because of bad weather or my faulty propeller, and then found myself again above enemy positions, everything looked different. Where should I begin to report the many changes that had occurred? How should I understand the maze of positions, encampments and ditches? I often felt discouraged. But only for a few moments. Then I took my pencil and started writing down my observations.

Soon, I thought of nothing else but the enemy and his location. This day there were new soldiers arriving at the British positions. Through my field glasses I could see bearded men with large khaki turbans unloading carts and setting up tents. I marked the location on my map."

His lengthy reconnaissance was ended on that particular day when five Japanese aircraft chased him back to base. They obviously did not want the German "Sky Spy" over their positions. The Nieuport monoplane must have had problems because it was not reported to have been airborne very often. This was fortunate for Plüschow as it was a much faster aircraft than the Farmans.

The maneuverability of the Rumpler-Taube, even with the faulty propeller, compared to the French Maurice-Farmans enabled Plüschow to elude his pursuers time after time. This was not lost on the early Japanese Air Corps design engineers, who, a few years before World War II, developed the highly maneuverable Mitsubishi "Zero" fighter plane.

The Japanese had installed a Hotchkiss type-3 heavy machine gun on the Farman three seater. The gun fired 6.5 mm rounds at 500 per minute. Since the bi-plane with the pusher-propeller had no obstruction from the large open front cockpit, the gun had a parabolic firing axis of half a circle. This plane had a pilot, a gunner and an observer. It also carried bombs and the additional weight reduced the speed and rate of climb.

Plüschow was not hit as he turned and dove like a moth darting from a swallow. He quickly learned that, flying below the Japanese, the machine gun could not be trained downwards. Also the enemy ground-fire dared not shoot at him lest they hit their own planes. He stuck close to them like a pilot fish next to a shark. When the Farmans finally broke off the chase, Plüschow flew in low between Bismarck and Iltis forts and landed amidst a barrage of artillery shrapnel and aerial bombs exploding all over the field.

The plane was immediately rolled under the protective over-hang of iron plates, dirt and brush. The automobile, protected by a plate-iron roof, hurriedly drove Plüschow through the rain of shrapnel to headquarters where he reported the news that scores of large siege guns were in fixed positions on cement platforms. (There were eventually over 140) There was also a massive number of troops, (over 37,000) and more men and supplies were steadily arriving.

Plüschow had just landed when at 9:00 a.m. the warships again began their heavy bombardment of the fort adjacent to his airfield. The day before on October 29, as if a signal to the Germans that the land bombardment and assault was imminent, the Anglo-Japanese Navy began a full-scale shelling of Hweichuen fort. The British battle-ship *Triumph* had been repaired and joined the *Suwo*, *Okinoshima* and *Tango* in lobbing shells from 9:30 a.m. until 4:30 p.m. Hweichuen fort fired sporadic responses, but couldn't reach the warships. The spotting station on Mt. Prinz Heinrich for the first time coordinated the firing by wireless. As the site was located ninety degrees to the line of fire, the spotting was considered effective. Admiral Kato was assured that the 197 shells fired that day had caused extensive damage.

In reality the bombardment had again done only slight dam-age. Several cracks appeared in the thick cement which sifted dust to the Germans deep below. The total damage was said to have been a rifle, two cartridge crates and several telephone lines exposed on the exterior. An enterprising German mathematician figured that the

Allied ships had wasted some two million marks in order to destroy property worth a hundred marks.

On October 30 the Japanese warships fired 240 shells. They determined the precise range of Hweichuen fort to be 14,130 meters. Moving their buoys to that distance, they fired with impunity. Their communication with the fire control station on Mt Prinz Heinrich was further perfected.

The Germans knew that the assault was imminent. They also knew that they could not hold out for long against the odds of some thirteen to one. Their ammunition was very low and because of this shortage, the batteries could only fire on some of the targets that Plüschow reported.

Meyer-Waldeck had ordered the sinking of their ships to block the harbor to prevent the Japanese from using it as spoils of war. On October 28, the steamer *Michael Jepsen* was sunk in the gap between two other vessels sunk previously on October 14. The entrance to the big harbor was now completely sealed.

The next day on October 29 when the naval bombardment was underway, the Germans moved the old disarmed gunboat *Tiger* out to a buoy in Kiaochow bay preparatory to sinking her. The Japanese land batteries started firing after the crew had left the ship. The range was a bit long for their guns, but they fired over 200 shells and after hitting her three times they stopped. A Chinese who had rowed out to the vessel, after the Germans left, apparently a looter, scurried off the ship in his sampan. His movement had been seen by the Japanese who believed the vessel was getting under way and that precipitated the attack. When it was dark the Germans sank the ship with explosives.

That same night a lone Japanese aircraft circled Tsingtau and dropped magnesium flares on selected targets before dropping bombs. In the hushed pause of the shelling, the foreboding sound of the explosions and the bright flares was like a starting signal. It was too dark to hardly see the aircraft, much less shoot at it. The setting moon showed enough distinguishing landmarks in the blacked out city.

There was a pattern to the bombing. The first one detonated almost on the power plant, then near the oil storage tanks, Bismarck barracks and the fort, then Moltke and Iltis forts, Signal Hill and the airfield. Plüschow and his plane had become an important target. Iltis Platz was distinguished by being given the last three bombs which again missed the Taube.

The aircraft was apparently marking the locations for fire control spotters. The mission completed, the sound of the airplane engine faded off into the distant silence. It was an ominously quiet and clear night of October 30, the first hard freeze of the season.

# CHAPTER 11

## PLÜSCHOW ESCAPES

The clear crisp dawn of October 31 predicted a warm day after the cold night. For the Germans it was just another Saturday. The men in the defensive positions had just completed their morning exercises and were lining up for hot coffee and bread. Some men were exercising or involved with their toilet, others taking a stroll and still others were eating breakfast. A dozen men were fishing in the harbor. The guns were silent. Everything was peaceful, quiet, calm. It was the Emperor's birthday.

The Japanese goal was to have already captured Tsingtau by this special day as a gift to the Mikado, but they had been thwarted for the most part by the weather and also by their wary respect for the German military machine. The Kaiser's successes in Europe against three major nations were well known.

High on Mt. Prinz Heinrich the Japanese in the observation post were watching the red ball of sun, their national symbol rise above the horizon of the Yellow Sea. At 6:10 a.m. the troops and artillerymen gave three hearty cheers of "Seiju no Banzai" (long live the Emperor) and General Watanabe's signal flare simultaneously fired his one hundred plus, siege guns.

The sound was deafening. In seconds the heavy shells exploded upon the Germans. All thoughts of food, fishing, walks, or cleanliness were forgotten. The men fled for protection into their redoubts, trenches and turtle-like fortifications.

Shortly after the barrage began, the Standard Oil storage tanks were hit and soon after, the tank of the Asiatic Petroleum Company.

They exploded in great sheets of flame. Billowing smoke rose straight up into the cloudless, windless sky and formed two giant black fists above the city. Burning oil poured through the streets of the native section setting fires everywhere they touched. The Chinese fled in panic. Many were seen burning like human torches before perishing. Over one hundred lost their lives and hundreds more were injured and burned. They were treated by the German medical units as best they could. Flames soon ignited the lumber yard, the docks and the coal storage area. All burned fiercely. The fire-fighters did their best, but the oil-fed infernos were beyond their control.

As if on cue Anglo-Japanese warships moved into range and started their contribution to the reduction of the German defenses. The eastern end of the German defenses nearest the coast were pounded, but their favorite targets were Hweichuen and Iltis forts. These guns and the fear of the mine fields still kept the Japanese and British vessels at a distance.

Each of the Japanese land guns had their own allocated sector. Within these areas the guns fired, then increased range 50 meters, fired, increased another 50 meters and fired again. Then they would repeat firing, decreasing their range to the original. Up and down the bombardment continued. Their accuracy was excellent. The fact that many shells failed to explode saved the Germans from total disaster.

Damage reports inundated Meyer-Waldeck's headquarters. The Austrian battery took two direct hits. The thirteen casualties were not the last losses of the day as the cannonade pounded the defenses. All of the batteries sustained casualties. Red cross trucks constantly ferried the wounded to the military hospitals. The design of the roads, cut several meters below ground level like giant trenches, saved many vehicles from being hit. Exploding shells soon cut most telephone contact beyond repair.

There was very little response from the defenders until noon when the Japanese firing slowed to a less regular pattern. Their large cannon and the hastily built platforms were feeling the strain. Several of the concrete foundations cracked badly and became unusable. One "Ginger-beer bottle" howitzer was badly breached as it fired and several of the gun crew were killed and injured.

It gave the Germans a chance to clear their guns from the debris for a response. Unless the enemy had made a direct hit, the antique guns were readied almost immediately for action.

There were no complex fire control systems or finely machined parts of the more modern weapons. The two sides traded heavy fire, but the Japanese were superior in both quality and quantity. The Japanese fired sporadically and wildly at everything that seemed like the enemy. Many shells fell into the city. In the late afternoon all the Japanese batteries resumed firing a heavy barrage. They pounded the environs for over an hour, damaging numerous buildings and frightening, injuring and killing the Chinese mercilessly.

By day's end the German position was in disarray. A dozen guns were out of action, communications were cut, human movement impeded, the trench line all but destroyed, and wire entanglements smashed. The Germans could only glumly and fearfully admire the forceful assault that celebrated the Emperor's birthday.

At night the Japanese changed from high-explosive shells to shrapnel which they exploded over the German positions precluding any opportunity for the defenders to clean up and repair the damage. The still raging fires outlined the city and the mountains.

There was one soft point in the German defenses because of an unfortunate accident that happened a few weeks previously just after dark on October 16. A sailor in Redoubt 5 dropped a heavy metal box cover on a magnesium flare setting it off. The chain reaction quickly ignited the other flares. The tremendous fire could not be contained and within three hours it reached the ammunition magazine. For two hours the fireworks display continued. Over 200,000 rifle and machine gun ammunition, several hundred hand grenades, 1500 light flares, dynamite, land mines, and other explosives lit up the night sky. The redoubt was all but destroyed. That night the Germans stood at full alert thinking that the Japanese would take advantage of the situation and assault the defenses. The Germans lost sleep. The disinterested Japanese instead waited until the artillery barrage could begin first before expending manpower. Their aircraft certainly must have seen the damage to this particular area and would concentrate any assault at Redoubt 5.

Plüschow kept on standby for the possibility of getting into the air whenever he could. He had taken refuge with his four-man flight crew in the basement of his villa. Fortunately one of the forty wells within the city was at the north end of his flying field not far from his residence. Plüschow had the foresight to have acquired quite a flock of egg-laying and eating chickens and a few ducks so the men didn't lack food.

Plüschow;

"Suddenly in the middle of the night, when we could hear and see that enemy storm-troops gathering, all our cannons started to fire and covered the enemy batteries and the approaching troops with their destructive fire. The effect of this shelling must have been disastrous for the Japanese. They did not storm us as it seemed they had planned. The Japanese learned their lesson. But in revenge eight horrible days and nights followed where the enemy artillery did not stop for one single minute. Under such heavy shelling, nobody ought to have remained alive, but miraculously our losses were slight. The Japanese artillery did an excellent job which was not surprising since many of their artillery officers had been trained by us in Justerbog. But their ammunition was bad, and this was the reason for our few losses."

It was reported that between 15 to 25 percent of the estimated 30,000 (possibly twice that) large Japanese shells fired, failed to explode. The amount of land-siege ammunition on hand from Japanese reports were over 120,000 rounds. This was based on 80 rounds per day, per cannon, for a total of fifteen days.

The dawn of November 1 opened with a "Sunday Drum Concert." The Germans didn't hold church services, but there were many who held their own personal prayer services. All morning the Japanese land artillery pounded the German line of redoubts. The fleet just off 'Burial Island' fired 112 large shells against targets within their range in the eastern sector. The fortifications were engulfed in blowing dirt, choking fumes and exploding metal.

At midday several cannon were shifted to other targets. The prime objective was the signal station. The Japanese landed four 150 mm shells on the building within a half hour. The Germans had vacated the area when the shelling began. Most of the structure as well as a large part of the extensive wireless antennae was destroyed. The shells also shredded the flagpole holding the battle flag. A sailor quickly put up a replacement flag on the stump of the mast. The wireless station could now only receive messages from the German owned steamship Sikiang in Shanghai, but was not able to transmit until a day later when the equipment was partially repaired.

That afternoon Meyer-Waldeck gave direct orders that the systematic destruction of excess equipment, machinery and some weapons should begin. Various gun crews blew up their guns as they expended their final shells and then marched off to the front lines. In the dock area, the huge heavy-lift crane along with one of the world's largest dry dock, tug boats and all the reserve naval equipment was blown up and destroyed. The several hundred men that manned the docks then joined the infantry.

That night the cruiser *Kaiserin Elisabeth* fired the last of her shells, (which would total some 3500) at the Japanese positions nearest the bay. In the dark, the moving target could not be located by the Japanese batteries. After the last shell was expended, Captain Makoviz moved the ship to the deepest water of the bay and prepared for her burial. All the men but ten were removed and sent to the defense line. At midnight when Meyer-Waldeck gave permission, the ship was then abandoned, blown up and sunk. After days of continuous bombardment, the power station was finally hit on November 3 and the city was plunged into darkness. Generators at Bismarck and Hweichuen forts and the redoubts along the front were still in limited use. Elsewhere candles and oil lamps were used which made it difficult for the hospitals and field dressing stations.

Plüschow:
"A few days later, our last ship, the brave small cannon boat *Jaguar* followed the Austrian cruiser. On November 5, I too had to destroy my biplane. With much hard work and ingenuity, I had built a large hydro-biplane with the help of the Austrian Lieutenant Clobuczar and mechanics and dock crews. It was constructed from spare parts and repaired sections of Muellerkowski's crashed Taube. It had just been completed, and I wanted to start flying it to continue my reconnaissance flights. I could no longer use my landing strip which only 4000 to 5000 meters from the enemy, was under constant artillery fire. But nothing came of my biplane. All our efforts had been in vain."

Lieutenant Clobuczar was an engineer who the flyer had known in Europe and who had worked in the Lohner aeronautical shop. He apparently became a ship's engineering officer. His knowledge of repairing Plüschow's damaged plane and designing and building a float biplane with only the help of mechanics and shipyard workers was truly amazing. It is a loss to historical knowledge that no more details were documented or photographs made of the German seaplane built during the siege of Tsingtau.

As Plüschow only made a passing mention of this venture, it was possible that he had persuaded the high command that the inner bay would make an ideal safe airfield. The intense shelling of his airfield had precluded any further flights. Building the plane certainly kept him and his crew from being sent to the front. He had proven that aerial reconnaissance was vital to the defense of the city.

As Plüschow was destroying his "home-made" double-decker float plane, the Japanese began the day with a new tactic. Instead of heavy artillery fire, the Germans heard the drone of three aircraft flying low over the city and military positions. They dropped leaflets.

This was the second time (Psych-war) propaganda material was dropped from an aircraft. The earliest mention was when Lieutenant Franz von Heddessen flew a Rumpler Taube over Paris on August 30, 1914 and dropped four explosive devices and a message. The note said that the German army was at the gates of Paris and it exhorted the people of the capitol to surrender. It caused much consternation to the French citizens, but of course it wasn't true. More important, the primitive bombs killed one civilian and wounded four others.

Many of the Japanese packages didn't break open upon impact and instead of having the propaganda destroyed, Meyer-Waldeck had them distributed as souvenirs. The handbills were dated October 30. (The day they were apparently printed)

"TO HONORED OFFICERS AND MEN OF THE FORTRESS":

*"It would be contrary to the will of God and humanity if the so far unused weapons, ships and other structures, not being of tactical importance, were to be destroyed and only with the envious intent that they would fall into the hands of the enemy."*

*"Although we cannot believe that officers and men who value chivalrous honor would realize such a thoughtless deed, we never-the-less take the liberty of expressing the above as our opinion."*

Siege Command.

NOTE: The above was written in incorrect German, containing numerous mistakes in syntax and spelling.

The Japanese planes must have seen and reported the Germans destroying everything of value. The Japanese said, "If the spoils of war were to be denied the victors, the Germans would pay dearly."

Four Japanese warships, the *Mishiuma, Okinoshina, Iwami* and *Tango* moved into Hai-hsi bay behind Cape Jaeschke for a different bombardment on Tsingtau. They fired together with all the land batteries on Tsingtau. Seventy five shells of the heaviest size fell on the city itself. At the offset a stray shell hit the fire-control station on Hweichuen Fort, killing seven men and wounding three. Another shell, failing to explode, hit a glancing blow on the base ring of the barrel of a 240 mm gun and jammed the traversing mechanism.

The bombardment caused more damage than all of the previous ones. Giant projectiles exploded buildings as though they were cardboard. Entire rooms and walls collapsed. House-sized smoking craters appeared in the streets. The ground shook in a continuous earthquake. Telephone and electric poles quivered like tuning forks. It soon became apparent by the sound, which shells were "Incoming Trunks or Suitcases" and which were "outward bound."

A few days earlier, the Haipo water works had been assaulted shortly after being supplied with food for the very hungry defenders. As the Germans were busily eating, the Japanese cleverly attacked the position immediately after the supply patrol departed. Covered by an artillery barrage, that precluded any reinforcements being sent, they captured the pumping station intact and took twenty-one prisoners. Without warning no one knew of the loss until the water taps went dry.

The city now didn't have the regular water supply or manpower to fight the numerous fires. There were only the 40 emergency wells in the city but without electricity to run the pumps many were useless. Only a few of the primitive hand-drawn wells could be used. Many homes and buildings burned to the ground without any attempt to put out the inferno. Only the distance between structures spared the city from burning totally.

In the Chinese sectors the problems were magnified because of crowded conditions and flimsy construction. The shells just collapsed the structures onto the citizenry who had sought shelter in basements and underground store rooms. The Japanese could have easily flattened the city should the struggle continue. But this was not their goal. Throughout Nov 5th, it was evident they were poised to storm the city. They were up against the outer wall of the "big ditch" having systematically exploded pathways through the mine fields. The Germans could hear them shouting orders, signalling with whistles and digging trenches. It is interesting to note that the Japanese used the same whistle signals from German drill manuals that they had learned from their instructors. Subsequently the Germans knew what they were going to do before they executed it.

For the Germans this was the last stand. There was little possibility for an extended defense effort. The men from all the units that had been destroyed were sent to the outer defense line with rifles and fixed bayonets. The men living like rats deep in their burrows were hungry and exhausted from the heavy pounding and had no illusions as to the outcome. Dysentery was rampant.

Meyer-Waldeck relieved many of the older reservists from duty and instructed them to change into civilian clothes. These were the businessmen, bankers and executives who would continue the future of Germany's commerce in the Far East. The Governor didn't want them to be captured by the Japanese.

A report from Redoubt 3 to their Commander-In-Chief exemplified the conditions along the defense line:

"The entire work shot to pieces; a hill of fragments without any defenses. The entire trench system is demolished; the redoubt is still intact, but everything else, including the explosives depot is destroyed. Only one observation post is usable. I shall hold the redoubts as long as possible."

Meyer-Waldeck knew the final assault would come within hours. Even the password for the next day, "For Emperor and

Country" revealed the German desperation and despondency.

That same afternoon, Nov 5, Plüschow had been summoned to headquarters by Meyer-Waldeck. The Commander-In-Chief gave him instructions to leave the city before it fell. He was to fly the very next morning to neutral Chinese territory the best way he knew how. Plüschow was given a passport both in Chinese and in German, several war diaries, official papers including deeds to various properties, personal letters and some symbolic articles such as the eagle fastening from the top of the flagpole that had been blown off during shell fire.

After Plüschow had been dismissed Meyer-Waldeck commented for the second time that he didn't believe the Japanese would ever let the flyer escape. He seemed a bit envious that he was not an aviator.

Plüschow describes it like this;

"That afternoon I stood before my Governor who told me:

"We are awaiting the main attack from the Japanese every minute. Try to leave the fortification tomorrow morning in your plane. I am afraid, however, that the Japanese will not give you enough time. May God protect you. And thanks for all you did for Tsingtau."

He shook my hand warmly. His ice-blue eyes had for a moment melted. Before mine did I saluted and replied,

"I report off duty." and was dismissed.

Then followed short good-byes from my superiors and comrades. A big pile of private letters and official documents were given to me. I was driven to my villa through the bombardment for the last time and said goodbye to my rooms and all the cherished objects. I opened the barn door to let out my horse and my chickens and ducks. Then I went to my plane to get it ready.

I studied the map, calculated, measured and memorized it

practically by heart. At night I went for the last time to my good friend, Naval Lieutenant Aye who had resisted for weeks the heaviest artillery shelling with his small battery. From his position one had a splendid view over Tsingtau and the surrounding area. I was overwhelmed; the flash of guns and explosions of shell fire looked like lightening flashes forming a golden band from sea to bay where all the artillery and machine guns were firing. Shells screamed overhead on their way to targets. Close by howitzers roared. Shrapnel grenades lit up the night and fragments fell like red-hot drizzle.

I felt horrible at the devastation and left after a brief handshake with Aye. I was the last officer in Tsingtau to see him. A few hours later, he fell against a 30 times stronger enemy. He and his small troop refused to surrender their position.

The rest of the remaining night I spent with my four brave assistants at my plane, so that I could execute my orders to take off immediately in case the Japanese would storm and reach us.

On November 6, 1914, very early in the morning when the moon was still shining brightly, my plane was ready to start. I stored letters, diaries and documents beside me and also in the front cockpit. The tank was full of benzin. There was no time to lose. The landing area had become dangerous because of the constant grenade and shrapnel shelling by the Japanese. The men had labored all night filling in the shell holes. I fastened my cap and goggles on my head, shook hands with my four brave assistants, hugged my dog, stroked his head goodby and climbed into the Taube. Then with the sailors holding the plane like a slingshot, I accelerated and the dove rose like an arrow into the air. The wind was from the north west and I was headed towards the battle line. I just began my turn at 30 meters when suddenly my plane received a terrible shock. Only barely could I control it and save from falling. An enemy grenade had exploded directly under me and the air blast from the detonation almost did me in. The enemy had seen me.

Except for a hole the size of a fist in my left wing, no damage was done. I turned hard left over Bismarck fort. My plane's left wing nearly touched the trees and rocks and the Christ Church steeple. I steered the wheel calmly. An extra intense volley of shrapnel exploded about me like brown-grey puffs, the last "regards" from the Japanese and their British allies.

When I was high in the air, I looked back once more. There was Tsingtau, my beloved second fatherland, a paradise on earth in flames. The sea of lightening flashes let me recognize the two firing lines and the beginning of the storm-attack. Would we be able to resist the third assault? My comrades were already burning and destroying the two hangers and the decoy plane. I waved goodby. On the Signal Station the war flag still waved from the wireless mast where it had been raised after the flagstaff had been shot away. The first light of the morning caught the red and white of the large red cross flags over the hospitals. Across the Yellow Sea the rays of gold were announcing the coming of the sun.

It was very difficult to gain altitude. The plane was heavy. I quickly turned to take a heading for Cape Jaeschke and dodged a lone carrier-pigeon flying to Tsingtau from the observation post. I felt sad I could not take the tiny Taube with me. When I had gained the altitude where the plane was invisible, I briefly circled the enemy ships cowering behind the protection of the islands and headland. By the time the sun rose, I was still climbing in the clear air and headed toward the jagged Pearl mountains and neutral China to the south. I had succeeded in running the Tsingtau blockade. I didn't look behind me again."

After passing the last obstacle; the mountains of Pearl, Plüschow flew down the coast at a height of 2000 meters. An hour later he passed over Japanese vessels gathered like scavengers around the carcass of the beached torpedo-boat *S-90*, His plan was to land at the town of Haichow just over the Shantung border in the province of Kiangsu, about 250 kilometers (155 miles) distant and thirty kilometers inland from the Yellow Sea. He might obtain fuel there and continue to Shanghai where he had friends. Flying in a primitive aircraft with a patched propeller high above a foreign country with a simple hand compass and map must have been as much of an adventure then, as today's probes into outer space.

When he reached his destination in two and a half hours, he couldn't locate a suitable landing site. The heavy autumn rains had flooded the whole country for many scores of kilometers. He flew on, but failed to locate a dry spot. When he was some 50 kilometers past his destination, he saw the thin silver line of the Grand Canal far to the southwest. It stretched one thousand kilometers through China from Tientsin to the Yangtze River, not far from the city of Nanking. If he had enough fuel he could have flown to Shanghai in another two and a half hours, but his fuel ration was down to one quarter. If he pressed onward he knew eventually he might be forced to descend in some out-of-the-way village, the inhabitants of which had never seen a white face, much less a flying machine. In Haichow, at least there was some sort of a civilization to be found, according to the travel-guide book; maybe even fuel. Plüschow turned and headed back.

Plüschow:

"I peered down between the wing and the body of my monoplane for a landing place but it looked as if I was to be disappointed. The rain of the past days had soaked the country and only the Chinese grave mounds, buildings and an occasional patch of high ground showed above the flood".

After some surveying, with his fuel gage almost on empty, he found a small field enclosed by ditches that looked as if it might have been drained into a state of comparative dryness. It was about 120 meters long and 18 meters wide flanked on one side by a deep river and on the other by the high walls of Haichow. He spiralled down to the four hundred by sixty foot space dragging his tail skid in the mud and keeping his wheels up until the last moment.

Plüschow:
"The landing was rather difficult but at 8:45 my machine stood in the middle of the field, at the last moment nearly capsizing for the wheels sank deep in the muddy ground and a propeller blade snapped short. For the first time in days I had landed without the accompaniment of crashing shells and whistling shrapnel. Peaceful and still my pigeon sat in the sun."

Plüschow disentangled himself from the plane, discovered that no bones were broken and looked about him. It was so quiet. The familiar roar of the Japanese artillery and the drone of his Taube was missing. Dogs barked and a cock crowed. From the houses in the distance he saw a crowd of Chinese running towards him. The silence didn't last long. Soon he was surrounded by a mob of jabbering, gesticulating Chinese who had never seen an aeroplane before and wondered what kind of a "Yang Kweitza" (foreign devil) had come down from the sky. His leather helmet and goggles must have given him the look of an alien from another world.

The pigtailed men kept the women and children behind them. At first they were too frightened to approach, but when he threw out a handful of copper coins and spoke a few words of the North Chinese dialect, they decided he was mortal. They hustled and jostled each other in their curiosity to examine the strange "Fei Ji" (fly-machine) But they kept at a distance, meanwhile grinning at the man who flew it and chattering loud remarks to the pilot and to one another.

No one seemed inclined to help him or even get too close. Suddenly he heard a strong voice in English say "Good morning." It was Doctor Lorenzo S. Morgan, an American missionary living in Haichow who had hastened to the assistance of the white aviator.

Plüschow, speaking good English, explained who he was and where he was from. After he crawled out, the missionary, speaking fluent Chinese, got some men to help right the plane. Plüschow then retrieved the satchel of documents, his Mauser pistol and removed the steering wheel for some reason unexplained as the plane was inoperative without a propeller or fuel. Perhaps he wanted it as a memento.

As Governor of Tsingtau, Alfred von Meyer-Waldeck had given Plüschow a passport written in both Chinese and German certifying his identity, nationality and where he was from. It also acknowledged that under International treaties, China being neutral, would have the obligation to intern him. The passport was sent by Dr. Morgan's messenger to the local Mandarin magistrate. Soon after, some forty-five soldiers came to guard the plane.

Plüschow enjoyed breakfast with Dr. Morgan and his wife and related his experiences as the one-man German air force, the "Dragon-Master of the Tsingtau Siege." Ruth Bennet Morgan was also a medical doctor and the second woman doctor to have graduated from Johns Hopkins in 1904. She was also an avid photographer and took many photos of Plüschow and his Taube. She had also been in Tsingtau in July when the plane was being assembled.

Plüschow:
"I cannot express strongly enough my appreciation of the kindness of the American missionaries at Haichow. When I flew out of Tsingtau, the only personal effects that I had with me were a piece of soap and a tooth brush. When I left

Haichow I needed four coolies to carry the provisions and other things that the missionaries gave me.

It was my intention to intern my Taube with the Chinese. But it was impossible to bring it, wings and all, through the gate of the walled city. I therefore removed the wings before burning the plane."

Even though he was placed in "protective" custody, Plüschow was treated like a very important person by everyone including the Mandarin, who gave a banquet in his honor. The flyer, now dressed in his civilian suit, demonstrated his good will by presenting his Mauser pistol and ammunition to the magistrate. Doctor Morgan suggested that Plüschow save the valuable engine. A day later he removed the engine and radiators after great difficulty and gave it to the same Chinese official. A photo taken by Doctor Ruth Morgan shows him doing this. Doctor Morgan suggested that the wings be removed and saved. The purpose; unclear except that Ruth Morgan saved a piece of the wing fabric as souvenir. There were other photos, taken by Ruth Morgan. SEE PHOTOS

An article regarding Plüschow's crash landing in Haichow was published by Doctor Morgan's son Carrel Morgan in Popular Aviation in 1938. He related to this author that Plüschow's light wooden seat with a cloth cushion was saved and he remembers sitting in it as a child in Haichow. Apparently there was no seat in the forward cockpit.

After the body was rolled in through the gate to a town square, Plüschow piled boxes around the plane and set the Taube's fuselage afire with the remaining fuel. Only the skeletal frames remained.

# CHAPTER 12

## FINAL HOURS—SURRENDER

After Pluschow had escaped, much to the chagrin of the Japanese, their Army and Navy Air corps spent the rest of the day bombing Tsingtau and the defenses. The effort was more psychologically effective than militarily. The land and sea bombardment was intensified throughout the day and into the late evening, when it abated.

Lt. General Kamio knew that the German training manual stated that the enemy's best time to attack was at dawn. But he believed in the Japanese "surprise-attack method." He also knew, because of the inactivity of the German troops at night, that they adhered to the manual.

The night of November 6 was clear and brightly moonlit. The Japanese officers had put on their "Shirotasuki" (a white band around their chest as a sign of acceptance of death in combat) and several thousand "Kesshitai" of a suicide detachment were ready to breach the walled ditch of barbed wire entanglements and mines.

The first serious engagement started at 9 p.m. around Redoubt IV. The probe was met head on by the Germans. Rifle fire being impracticable at night, the garrison had been provided with improvised grenades with 3 centimeter short fuses a little over one inch. Lit with a special match, the grenades were held for a count of three and then thrown; hardly any were returned by the Japanese. The fierce struggle was a brief one and fought with fists, bayonets and rifle butts. The Germans succeeded, and the Japanese retreated. The Japanese commander was wounded and sent out calls for support, but none arrived. When he and his men had to climb back up the outer wall of the "ditch" German searchlights made them easy targets against the white-washed cement. A considerable number were left dead or dying on the entanglements.

The attack on Redoubt III is described in much greater detail by a Japanese officer. The 56th Japanese Infantry, with the 2nd and 3rd battalions in the first line had occupied trenches within ten meters of the crest of the first glacis. While the Japanese were being repulsed at Redoubt IV, the engineers cut two lanes about five meters wide through the wire.

At 7:00 P.M. Second Lieutenant Nakamura reported to battalion headquarters. He at once assembled his squad leaders and gave the following orders:

"Uniform light order. Leave off knapsacks. Put one day's ration of toasted bread in the packs. Carry full canteens and haversacks. Wear as clean underwear as possible. Leave behind handbooks, diaries, etc., and all men will tie a white band around the left arm, the "Shirotasuki." Arms will be rifles, bayonet, entrenching tools and 210 rounds of ammunition. I will carry a white flag, and each man will carry a national flag."

Nakamura then received instructions at battalion headquarters. A sergeant and 20 men from the Engineers, and three sergeants and three lance corporals especially selected from the 3rd Battalion were attached. He was given 30 hand grenades and a field signal lantern. He was told that the artillery would cease fire during the charge, but would open up during the pursuit. An infantry squad and two mortars would provide cover to the north and south. The battalion and regiment would be in position to advance at the proper time.

He returned to his platoon, instructed his men in the use of the

156

grenades and signal lantern and addressed the men as follows:

"It is essential, but most difficult, for military men to find a fit place in which to die. That we have been selected from the entire army to charge and capture the central position is a very great honor. Since our departure from Japan we, of course, have always had the resolution to do or die...."Shirotasuki!" It is considered a disgrace for military men to be captured or die of disease during a march or while besieged. You will be spared this." The Lieutenant continued:

"Tonight I will offer my life to the Emperor. Life or death is ordered by Heaven and is beyond the power of man. To meet death composedly when it comes is the special characteristic of our country's warriors. This platoon must capture the central fort tonight, regardless of circumstances. Ground once captured must not be yielded even one step. If I fall the squad leader takes my place; if he falls the lance corporal takes command; if he falls all must cooperate and fight furiously even to the last man.

Rifles will not be loaded, because as soon as we see the enemy we must jump at him with the bayonet. As soon as we meet the hostile machine guns, the hand grenades will be thrown and we will charge just they explode. The men who carry them will advance at the head of the platoon. Volunteers for this duty will report to me."

The entire platoon stepped forward as one man. Ten were selected and each one put three grenades in his outer pockets. On command from the company commander, who was also present, the platoon faced in the direction of the Imperial Palace, presented arms with fixed bayonets, and marched off silently.

Redoubt 3 had been pounded extra heavily during the day. Counter to the German battle strategy, the defenders didn't think that the Japanese would attack at night, especially after they had been so badly repulsed at Redoubt 4.

Promptly at 1 A.M. the ladders were lowered, the ditch quietly crossed and the detachment arrived under the enemy parapet. Lance Corporal Shima immediately signalled to the rear. Everything was so quiet inside the fort that it seemed like it was a trap. During this time the Engineers had cut all telephone wires they had located and forced their way into the telephone station. The Germans inside on duty tried to resist with pistols, but they were overcome without firing a shot. The confusion of the enemy as they jumped out of bed, was hard to describe. After a brief but overwhelming hand-to-hand combat, the Germans surrendered after sustaining numerous losses and being blasted with hand grenades.

Later it was learned that the German sentry had at first thought the detachment only a small patrol, and realized his mistake too late when he was bayoneted. One hundred and thirty men were captured in Redoubt III.

By this time the entire defense line had been alerted and were attempting to repulse the enemy. As soon as the search lights were turned on the mirrors were shot out. There was no time to replace them. The barbed wire that was left was now breached with explosives on poles. Heavy bamboo matting was thrown onto the top of the wire. More ladders scaled the walls. Hoards of Japanese poured over the top. They had made a major breakthrough. Troops streamed double time through the breach two abreast, like ants streaming to an ant-hill.

At about 3 in the morning the Japanese began firing into the rear of the line of redoubts, now completely surrounded. The bomb-proof bunker at Redoubt IV was blown up. Meyer-Waldeck ordered a concentrated last-effort attack with all the artillery available. The guns fired their last rounds at short range and were blown up by propelling charges as ordered. With screams of "Banzai" the troops overwhelmed the German positions one by one. Many Japanese trying bravely to stop the Germans from destroying their guns lost their lives in the explosions.

The Japanese bombardment and assault of Tsingtau was described by a British officer of Marines as "a wonderful sight, and the Japanese shooting as magnificent."

"There is hardly a stick left in the forts and redoubts — concrete platforms, trenches, guns and barbed wire entanglements blown to atoms. The bombardment continued for a week, and during that time the Japanese and British dug trenches till they were right up and half round the German forts; the "square-heads" put up the white flag when they saw a chance of getting a bayonet stuck in them. There is no doubt the Japanese are wonderful soldiers."

Finally at 6:23 in the morning of November 7, 1914, the Governor, with the consensus of his staff, surrendered Tsingtau. White flags were hoisted on signal hill and several fortified positions. A communique of surrender was drawn up. It translated:

"Your Excellency!
*Since my defensive means are exhausted, I am now ready to enter into surrender negotiations for the now open city.*

*If your Excellency agrees to this proposal, I request you to appoint plenipotentiaries to the discussions, as well as to set time and place for the meeting of the respective plenipotentiaries. For my part I will appoint as chief negotiator the Chief of Staff, Captain Saxer."*
The Imperial Governor
Meyer-Waldeck

This communique was carried to the commanding Japanese General by Major von Kayser riding on horseback with a bugler carrying a white flag and a horse-holder. The small party rode out bravely into the continuing battle, searching for a route through the chaos.

Near the village of Tai-tung chen, they soon were caught in the crossfire between the lines. At first the Japanese refused them passage. The Germans waved their arms and yelled, while the bugler blew the call for cease fire. Stray bullets killed the unarmed horse-handler and shot the horse from under von Kayser.

After a long delay, they received Japanese permission to proceed to the same place where von Kayser had negotiated the cease fire on October 13th. In a hurried exchange, the two sides agreed to a general armistice and to begin the formal surrender meeting that afternoon at Moltke barracks. Bismarck barracks was still burning badly.

Despite the cease fire agreement, the battle raged on. The windless day left the white flags hanging limp. Telephone lines had mostly been destroyed. Meyer-Waldeck sent out five motorcycle riders with surrender messages, but they were all captured by the Japanese who couldn't understand them.

Redoubts I and V refused to surrender and in desperation Meyer-Waldeck dispatched staff messengers on foot to relay the cease fire order. Finally as the news circulated among the defenders, the sounds of battle finally stopped. The last sound of battle was a German light artillery shell which killed two British soldiers preparing to march into the city.

The surrender had caught General Kamio by surprise. He had not been ready for a triumphant entrance into the city. But the British were. The Japanese had not given the Borderers much participation in the final assault and they were better organized to take over Tsingtau. They were ordered to march into the city by Barnardiston at 7:30 a.m. But they were delayed an hour. Lieutenant H.W. Beaumont Walker had put his wet trousers on a parapet to dry the night before. When the order came to march, he couldn't put on his frozen uniform until he finally managed to struggle into the half-thawed garment. Because of this humorous incident, his platoon came last in line rather than leading the British contingent.

Finally at 8:30 a.m. the British troops were marching four abreast into the city much to the irritation of the Japanese. They passed a German prisoner column who immediately turned their backs and as the British passed, bent over displaying their naked buttocks. The Japanese guards laughed gleefully at the incident, further embarrassing the Britishers marching "ever so properly."

But the Japanese also got even with the Britishers. When the surrender document was signed, first by the Japanese and then the Germans, no one asked for the British signature. It was only noted that the British representative Lieutenant Colonel Calthrop was present. The Japanese did not even inform General Barnardiston that the formal surrender was taking place, much less ask his participation. The weak British military contribution during the siege gave them a humiliating "lose face" status in the Far East. They never did regain "face."

The friction between the Japanese and British continued even after the surrender. The Japanese Emperor ordered that the German officers be allowed to keep their swords. Major General Yamanashi in a theatrical proclamation stated that the gracious allowances came from the Emperor himself. The British officer Calthrop interjected;

"I also have the honor to report that through the generosity of my sovereign, the German officers may retain their swords."

This proved too much for the Japanese officer who caustically responded, "Can you show me the paper authorizing this expression of your King's will?"

Needless-to-say he couldn't. This cutting put-down was widely reported in the German and American press per reports of the Associated Press correspondent A.M. Brace.

Otto Wiesinger, a reservist who was hospitalized with acute dysentery, says in his memoirs;

"Around seven o'clock in the morning we saw the first invading Japanese through the windows of our military hospital. Divided into smaller units, swinging small Japanese flags, they roamed through the various parts of the city and immediately made ready to occupy all important positions. At the sight of them, many of the nurses at the hospital broke out in loud sobs."

"It was not long before ambulances arrived, delivering German and Japanese soldiers, without distinction. Then a car arrived across whose seats two Japanese soldiers lay. Their legs hung down on each side. They were unconscious. Two badly wounded men! Carefully the two warriors were lifted onto stretchers. The operating room was made ready. As the men were being inspected, it came as a complete surprise that there were no wounds visible on either man. Only then it became evident that not only there was nothing amiss with them except that they were dead drunk!"

Wiesinger goes on to say:

"It can be said, in general, that the behavior of the Japanese soldiers was exemplary. While there were a few cases of looting during the invasion of the city after its storming, the Japanese command moved with extreme severity against anyone who was caught in any disorderly action. In fact, the Indian troops, under English command, behaved far more badly in this respect."

Another report by Vollerthun, "In Kampfum Tsingtau", page 171 differed in tone from the man in the hospital who apparently was well treated.

"Small groups of Japanese soldiers appeared in city streets, followed soon after by cavalrymen riding through the city. They quickly rounded up about a hundred old reservists who had been acting as policemen. These elderly men quickly surrendered their weapons to the scowling battle-dirty victors. Without any symbol of authority, the soldiers began entering homes and looting those items they could carry, particularly money which there was only little of. During this looting some Japanese found caches of alcohol and began mistreating and man-handling civilians. These isolated incidents started wild rumors throughout Tsingtau. But in short order the Japanese command disciplined the troops responsible and moved most of them out of the city."

Kurt Schultze-Jenn, "Der Kamf um Tsingtau" Verlag Nossler, Shanghai 1915, page 18.

"The Germans, in a final rush of destruction, destroyed even the paper money in the bank, postal stamps, the official papers in the city record files and all battle-flags. The Germans left very little for the conqueror."

The Japanese counted 2,300 prisoners that day plus what they had captured during the siege. In the late afternoon the Germans were marched inland. They were allowed a blanket or coat and only personal effects that could be carried. The older reservists who could afford it were allowed to have rickshaw men carry their baggage. It was a somber procession through the still burning city on the way to Lao Shan harbor where the Japanese ships were to take them to Japan. Once outside the defense zone, the Japanese guards lodged their prisoners in Chinese villages. The inhabitants were rudely ejected from their houses to sleep outside in the freezing weather or find whatever shelter they could.

On November 9th, Meyer Waldeck was allowed to send the following telegram to the Kaiser;

"After exhausting all means of defense at its command, the fortress fell after being stormed and breached at the center. The fortress installations and the city were badly damaged after being shelled with heavy artillery up to 28 cm together with a heavy bombardment from the sea. Finally, the artillery power of the fortress was completely broken up. Losses cannot yet be calculated accurately, but, as if by a miracle, are far less then was to be expected in view of the extremely heavy and continuing fire."

The Kaiser responded through the American Embassy in Berlin with his recognition for their faithful service and with the award of the Iron Cross, First Class for Meyer-Waldeck.

Shortly the Japanese Red Cross Society took over the administration of the military hospitals. At that time the following printed announcement was handed to each patient:

TO THE GERMAN WOUNDED AND SICK IN TSINGTAU:

"We, the medical corps of the Japanese Red Cross Society have been sent here on order of the Minister of War to administer to your wounded and sick, who have fought faithfully and bravely for the fatherland.

As is well known to you, the Red Cross strives for universal humanitarianism. We will now attempt to put into practice this spirit and principle. You will please note that our medical ministrations in Tsingtau are naturally being carried out on order of the Imperial Japanese Military Authorities.

We are pleased to remember that, in the earlier war, we received much and grateful sympathy from all parts of Germany. This expedition also represents our return service for this, and we hope, therefore, that you will be frank and sincere towards us.

Finally, we hope that you will soon recover completely from your ailment."

Y. TANAKA, Director of the Japanese Red Cross Society.

On November 9 the Germans were allowed to have a collective afternoon burial service attended by civilians and a few military as described by Otto Wiesinger just out of hospital.

"It was an unusually lovely autumn day on November 9 when great numbers of non combatant German men, women and children swarmed out to the cemetery, ideally located at Iltis Platz a few score of meters from Plüschow's still smoldering hanger. Golden rays of sun shone onto the graves which were decorated with fresh greenery and wreaths. Paster Winter and Father Schoppelrey presided.

With emotional fervor the minister described the devotion with which the brave warriors, true unto death, had given their lives for the fatherland:

"Never will perish that which German industry and German

culture have accomplished here during years of hard work... Tsingtau is German and remains German."

An honor guard fired three salvoes, careful since they used live ammunition. Then they handed over their rifles to the Japanese soldiers, who signaled the end of the ceremony with a brusque wave of their weapons. The bell in the Christ Church tolled the last farewell. The most moving experience for all was a widow with her three children mourning her reservist husband.

The following day the defeated Governor met Kamio at Moltke Barracks. As Meyer-Waldeck walked past a Japanese honor guard, the men snapped to rigid attention. The Japanese Commander-in Chief arrived on horseback. Over champagne and cigars he expressed carefully phrased regrets and sorrow over the conflict through two interpreters. It was a pleasant three-quarter hour conversation made even more pleasing to the Germans by the deliberate inattention to Calthrop, who represented the British.

Kamio reiterated the debt of the Japanese military leaders to their German teachers and he expressed his hope that the two armies, which had worked together so well in the past, would be able to do so again. Twenty-five years later the Axis Powers were formed, which included Japan and was headed by Germany!

Only three days after the surrender, Takahashi opened his photography shop on what was previously called Friedrich Strasse. All German streets, buildings and Chinese villages were given Japanese names. New currency was introduced. Military police patrolled the city. The Diedrichs stone monument on signal hill commemorating the occupation of Tsingtau in November 1897 with the crest of the Imperial Eagle, was chiseled over with the Japanese inscription "In the third year Taisho on November 7th. 1914"

The Anglo-Japanese fleet had fired some 1,118 shells to silence two guns, one claim of which was questionable. One report stated that 2000 rounds of 7.5 inch caliber or larger were fired by the fleet knocking out only the fire-control station and one gun on Hweichuen point. This was the glancing blow of a dud on the base ring of a gun barrel. Most of the damage to the other forts was done by the Germans just before they surrendered. SEE PHOTOS

The Japanese never reported the total number of rounds fired from their 280 mm, 155 mm and 120 mm siege guns. But if each of the one hundred cannon (some reports say 140) fired only 70 shells a day, (one every 20 minutes) for an average of six days, the conservative total would be 58,800 rounds. (It could have been even more than that).

The casualties were not indicative of a huge conflict, but there are discrepancies in the reports. One historian states the Germans lost 199 killed and 294 wounded. The Japanese dead 415, and 1451 wounded, although there is one report that at the end of September, a month before the heaviest assault, the Japanese casualties were 1784 killed and some 800 wounded. Then other reports from an eye witness Otto Wiesinger said there were 210 Germans killed or died, 550 wounded. Taking this last and highest estimate by counting all cases of casualties and illnesses, estimated at 150, the German casualties numbered about 900 men or 20 percent of the garrison. From statements made privately by Japanese officers, their total military losses exceeded 12,000 men including many cases of dysentery. The British had 13 killed and 61 wounded; Sikhs only 2 killed and 4 wounded.

The Japanese Army Air Corps had made a total of 86 sorties; logged a total of 89 hours of flight time; dropped 44 bombs in 15 bombing sorties. The navy planes made a total of 49 sorties; logged a total of 71 hours of flight time and dropped 199 bombs. There was no exact record of the number of sorties Pluschow flew; the best estimate was 30 to 35. He dropped about 10 "bombs," claiming to have blown up a Japanese command center and shot down one plane. The command center claim is highly unlikely according to all historical reports except that Japanese were secretive about their damage reports and casualties.

166

It was reported that after the Japanese had stormed the installations they were very surprised to find such a small number of defenders in the redoubts. They found only 65 men in redoubt III and would not believe that this could have been the entire crew. They were so suspicious, they even tested the walls of the infantry installations on the assumption that some Germans might still be hidden within.

They were also surprised to find that their bombardment did such little damage to the heavy ferro-concrete fortifications. For the most part, the German guns had been deliberately blown up, but the published pictures led everyone to believe that the Japanese shells caused the damage.

Even the reports and photos of the sunken ships, demolished drydock and giant crane were attributed to Japanese fire power. What was certain was the thousands of unexploded shells that attested to the poor quality of Japanese munitions. Clean up by demolition squads were still being undertaken even eight months later, with scores of accidents and casualties.

The point of view of a British observer in an article by Major E.F. Knox, 36th Sikhs, in the Journal of the United Service Institution of India, February 2, 1915, states:

"A few words on our Allies may not be amiss. A point especially noticeable is the thoroughness in all their preparations for war... Their officers appear to leave little to be desired in either efficiency or military skill.

Perhaps the worst fault of the Japanese soldier, in non-commissioned ranks, is his appalling carelessness in dealing with explosives. After the fall of Tsing-Tao parties used to be sent out to collect live shells, unexploded hand grenades, etc. These they would dump into the botton of a cart without any precautions and the cart would then be taken across the roughest of country, at a gallop as likely as not, with fused thirty centimeter shells rattling together like so many loose peas. It was not surprising that fatal accidents were numerous."

The rest of the surviving Germans, as prisoners-of-war, were shipped to Japan on November 14 to be interned for the duration. As Meyer-Waldeck boarded the old coal vessel *Satsuma Maru* for the trip to Japan, he remarked that this day was 17 years to the day after the Germans had landed and taken over Tsingtau.

The Allied victory parade occurred on November 16 with the British units led by Barnardiston lost in the rear among the Japanese troops. The parade went through what was left of the city to Iltis Platz. Here on the assembly ground between the two ruins of Pluschow's hangers had been erected a vertical needle-like wooden monument. General Kamio presided at the ceremony. He read from a scroll indicting Germany for forcing the conflict and praising his army and thanking his fallen men.

Two days later the British Borderers and Indian Sikhs were ordered by the Japanese to leave Tsingtau. This caused great consternation to the Chinese Government. They hoped that with the British still having a toe-hold in Tsingtau, the Japanese could be persuaded to return the territory to China. Instead, the Japanese closed the port to all but their own shipping and imported over 10,000 Japanese citizens to colonize the city. About 250 German civilians were allowed to remain. The American consul Willys Peck soon reopened his office. The former British vice-consul Eckford, upon returning, found a Japanese flag flying outside his former house which was occupied by military officers. He diplomatically found quarters elsewhere.

Despite the destruction, Tsingtau was a great prize for the Japanese who refused to return it to China until forced to do so in 1922 through International pressure, mostly by the United States.

After the Armistice in 1918 a number of Germans returned to live and raise families in Tsingtau. This author knew several veterans during his 17 years there and was "ear-witness" to many firsthand accounts besides having often visited and explored the fortifications.

Hweichuen fort was retained as a war memorial and tourist attraction. For years after the war, the Japanese military studied the Tsingtau fortifications to learn how a few Germans, many only reservists, were able to defend against such great odds and massive bombardment.

In all there were some 60,000 Japanese and British both on land, sea and air against less than 4500 Germans, of which only 4,000 were proficient to fight...nearly a fifteen to one ratio!

The Hweichuen Fort was still there in 1949 when Mao's "Peoples Army" captured Tsingtau. Today the port is a major Chinese city and industrial center with over 23 times the 1914 population; now 1,500,000 people with another 4.5 millions in Greater Tsingtao. The fate of the Hweichuen war memorial fortress is unknown at this writing.

However, the author had the occasion to meet a Chinese business lady in 1993 visiting the United States from Tsingtau. She was born there and attended college there. When asked about the fort and shown pictures of 1914 to 1941 vintage, she was surprised at not knowing the past history of the German colony and the siege except to say that the point of land was a restricted military zone. "There is heavy fencing and guarded gates which keeps it off limits to casual visitors".

A recent U.S. Defense Mapping Agency chart No. 94283 of the harbor of "Qingdao Gang" (from China charts to 1986) shows nine prominent structures at the site of the old German fortifications at Hweichuen Point. Militarily experienced readers can more accurately "surmise" what is now there on that strategic point of land guarding the entrance to Kiaochow Bay. If the Germans once knew the importance of this piece of China and acquired the area for a major naval base... but no more need be said.

After obtaining brochures, post cards and tourist information, including a current documentary video on Tsingtau, it is odd that there is no mention or picture of this former fort except for very distant views. It must be noted that the current Chinese photographers made an apparent and determined effort to avoid Hweichuen Point as did the Germans when they were in control. The then popular Edgewater Hotel built at the neck of the peninsular in the mid 1930's, including the yacht club next to it, is still there. It is apparent that the current Chinese government simply erased past history. They erased something else.

The small German cemetery at Iltis Platz below Plüschow's former villa was tended by a Chinese gardener who was paid by the German government until the Chinese Communists dismissed him in 1949. Then it was tended by Fred Bischof a veteran who had settled in Tsingtau and married a Chinese woman. The Communists would not let him leave, but did allow him to do the work. Later, after they transferred him to another location, his Chinese wife with considerable difficulty, traveled to Tsingtau each November 7 to clean up the burial ground and to put flowers on the graves. In 1966, during the "Cultural Revolution" the graves were removed to an undisclosed location and the area bulldozed for a new housing project.

The Anglo-Japanese refused to concede that one of the reasons for the early surrender was that the Germans simply ran out of ammunition for their big guns. Both Japanese and British official reports and newspaper accounts erroneously stated that there was plenty of ammunition and food supplies for 5000 men for six months; food yes, ammo no.

While this Lilliputian struggle was not as large as the European conflict, it was historically more significant. The sleeping monster of Japan's ambitious militarism had been aroused. This battle field "laboratory experiment," tested nearly every known piece of equipment and technique of modern warfare, except chemical. The lessons learned were invaluable to Japan and the few International military observers who were able to circumvent the Japanese restrictions.

Most notable was the recognized contribution of air power. Planes had been used, not only for reconnaissance, but for bombing and air-to-air combat. The refinements of the Japanese use of airpower was far advanced to that of other nations in 1914. The first use of planes attacking warships and ground positions provided a tantalizing sketch for future Japanese strategic military scenarios; next practiced against Manchuria in 1932 and China from 1937 to the end of World War Two. But it's crowning aerial attack was against the United States at Pearl Harbor in 1941, which was also the falling curtain on the scenario of Japanese militarism.

To reiterate: This little known Far Eastern military campaign of World War One was credited with ELEVEN significant historical "FIRSTS", SIX of which were aviation firsts.

1. First German warplane to crash in China during a reconnaissance flight.
2. First seaplane carrier used in combat; Japanese.
3. First substantial size aerial bombs (with fins) dropped by the Japanese Navy on German forts and warships.
4. First air-to-sea engagement; Japanese planes vs German ships.
5. First "stealth" aircraft used in combat; the German Taube which was invisible at an altitude of 305 meters (1000 feet).
6. First night bombing initiated by the Japanese.
7. First capture of German territory by the Japanese.
8. First time Caucasian troops were under the command of Asiatics.
9. First British army commander to step on German soil; WW I.
10. First major loss of German colonial territory in World War I.
11. First combination of Land, Sea and Air Forces employed together in warfare.

NOTE:

(Possible) FIRST air-to-air combat with firearms. This "first" was disputed by an ambiguous back-dated French communique issued two months (Nov 1914) after the above report from Tsingtau was received in Europe.

(Possible) FIRST anti-aircraft fire-control mechanism devised and used by the Germans against the Japanese. The rapid-fire artillery removed from the Austrian cruiser *Kaiserin Elisabeth* were aimed with a state-of-the-art combination of range-finders, sextants and slide rule verniers. The instruments and schematics were destroyed in the siege.

\*\*\*

The vessels used in the blockade and bombardment of Tsingtau were the following:

| Battleships | Major Armament | Secondary Armament |
|---|---|---|
| *Suwo* (flagship) | four, 10 inch | ten, 6 inch |
| *Iwami* | four, 12 inch | six, 8 inch |
| *Tango* | four, 12 inch | twelve 6 inch |
| *Okinoshima* | three, 10 inch | four 4.7 inch |
| *Mushima* | four, 9 inch | four 4.7 inch |
| *Triumph* (British) | four, 10 inch | fourteen 7.5 inch |

Armored Cruisers; *Chiotose, Akashi, Akitoushim, Ghiveda, Iwate, Yakumo, Tokiwa.*

Light Cruisers; *Tone, Megami, Yedo, Akashi, Takachiho* (topedoed).

Gunboats; Seven, including five formerly Russian.

Destroyers; Sixteen, including the *Usk* & *Kennet* (British).

In addition there was a destroyer depot ship; a repair ship; a hospital ship (British); a surveying ship; 13 converted steamers and other craft for mine sweeping and a sea-plane mother-ship with a detachment of the Navy Air Corps consisting of 4 float planes.

JAPANESE NAVAL LOSSES;
* 1 Destroyer grounded and destroyed by German shell fire.
* 1 Aircraft mother-ship struck a mine and was beached.
* 1 Trawler aiding the aircraft vessel struck a mine and sank.
* 1 Trawler struck a mine the next day and sank.
* 1 Light cruiser *Takaschio* (1885 vintage) torpedoed, total loss.
* 1 Torpedo boat struck a mine and sank 3 days after the siege.
* 1 Mine sweeper struck a mine and sank after the siege.   A total of SIX vessels were completely destroyed.

*****

Most of the German Asiatic Fleet had been deployed to the Pacific leaving only small and obsolete warships that were noteworthy in their commendable performances.   They were:
Cruiser *Kaiserin Elizabeth* (Austrian-Hungary) built 1890, Length 351 feet; Main battery, two 7.5 inch and eight 6 inch.
Light Cruiser *Cormorant*.
Gunboats; *Tiger, Luchs, Iltis, Jaguar*.
Destroyer; *Taku*.
Torpedo-boat Destroyer *S-90* [four torpedo tubes]
Minelayer; *Lauting*
River gunboats; *Vaterland* and *Otter*;
also a captured Russian steamer.
All vessels were sunk or beached and blown up (*S-90*) by the Germans to blockade the harbor and to keep them from falling into the hands of the Japanese.

\*\*\*\*\*

The Japanese land forces, under command of Lieutenant General Kamio included the following units;
18th Division  (23rd and 24th Brigades)
29th Brigade
Siege Artillery Corps
Detachments of Engineers
Detachments of Army Service Corps, 6th and 12th Divisions
Two Railway Battalions
8th Infantry Regiment (Railway Guards)
Marine Artillery Detachment
Detachment of the Army Flying Corps with 5 planes.

\*\*\*\*\*

[These following numbers were obtained from two sources and differ slightly]  The German forces consisted of:
III SeeBatalion:

| | | |
|---|---|---|
| 4 Infantry companies | 1000 Officers & men | |
| 1 Militia company | 250 " | " |
| 1 Substitute reserve & Volunteer Co. | 300 " | " |
| 1 Mounted company | 200 " | " |

East Asian Marine Detachment:

| | | |
|---|---|---|
| 3 companies | 500 " | " |

Pioneers:

| | | |
|---|---|---|
| 1 company | 150 " | " |

Fifth Naval artillery:

| | | |
|---|---|---|
| 4 companies | 750 " | " |

Field artillery:
    1 company (6 quick firing 7.7-cm canons) 133  "     "
Field Howitzer Unit:
    3 guns                         30    "     "
Engineer Unit:
    1 company                   108    "     "
Machine gun Unit:
    12 Horse-drawn machine guns    77   "     "

Military Bureau:                    70   "     "

General staff, Intelligence: Signal & Wireless Telegraph Station, Fortification Department, Naval Bureau, Ordnance Department, Mine Department, The Observatory.
Flying Corps detachment: (Intelligence)
    2 Rumpler-Taube aircraft (1 crashed)  7 men

Balloon detachment: (Intelligence)
    2 Balloons (1 shot down and 1 adrift)  8 men

The ships complement totaled over 1100.

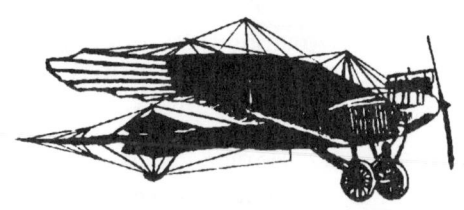

# EPILOGUE

## PLÜSCHOW'S ESCAPE FROM CHINA;
## ESCAPE FROM ENGLAND;
## POST WAR ADVENTURES.

During this time, the "Dragon Master's" adventures had not ended. After several days as "guest" of the Mandarin magistrate in Haichow, and having been feted and treated like a celebrity, he was transported to Nanking. "Just a formality," they told him. Plüschow was escorted by General Liu, a renowned fighter of pirates and bandits, his two officers and forty five soldiers. Plüschow was not dressed for this cold weather and was given clothing and a sleeping bag by Doctors Lorenzo and Ruth Morgan and a lot of provisions mentioned before.

The transportation from Haichow was by river to the Grand Canal that passed ninety kilometers away.

Plüschow:
"I started out on a Chinese river sampan pulled by coolies. A general and forty five soldiers accompanied me. After six days on the river and two along the Grand Canal we finally arrived at Nanking."

When they arrived at the Grand Canal and boarded a large two masted sailing Junk, the light breeze was from the wrong direction to use the sails. Several boatmen, with ropes harnessed to them pulled the vessel along the waterway. Eventually the junk hoisted the large square matting sails to catch the favorable wind. The trip took a total of eight days to travel the 250 kilometers, that Plüschow could have flown in two and a half hours. In contrast, today's fighter planes, only eighty years later, can fly the same distance in less than seven minutes! Arriving in Nanking Plüschow met "KapitanLeutnant" Brunner and the crew of the torpedo-boat *S-90* in the custody of the authorities. They had made the long trek over the mountains and then by train guarded by Chinese soldiers.

When Plüschow learned that he was really to be interned for the duration of the war even though the conditions were merely "house arrest" with two guards accompanying him whenever he wished to leave the premises, he decided to escape.

Since all foreigners looked the same to Orientals, Plüschow was able to fool his guards into believing that another German from the torpedo-boat was actually him. He made his way to Shanghai by train actually sitting in a compartment with a Britisher and passing himself off as a Swiss businessman.

In Shanghai he met the only other German, besides the ship's crew, who had escaped from Tsingtau; A 30 year old reservist and non-commissioned officer who had fled from a Tsingtau hospital. Otto Wiesinger, who had been a former import-exporter in Shanghai, and others helped Plüschow obtain a forged passport and money. Under the new identity of a "Mr. McGarvin," representative of the Singer Sewing Machine Company, Plüschow then booked passage to the United States aboard the American ship *Mongolia* which was to leave on December 5th.

The ship was scheduled to stop in Nagasaki, Kobe and Yokohama. Plüschow confided to the ship's American doctor who he actually was. In order to escape the scrutiny of the Japanese authorities, the doctor verified that Mr. McGarvin was sick and bed-ridden with food poisoning.

The American war reporter A.M. Brace, who had been in Tsingtau until after the surrender, was also aboard the ship. He was careful not to associate with the German flyer until after the ship left Japan.

The S.S. *Mongolia*, enroute to San Francisco, arrived in Honolulu on December 22, 1914. The following day the Pacific Commercial Advertiser, Honolulu published the following story.

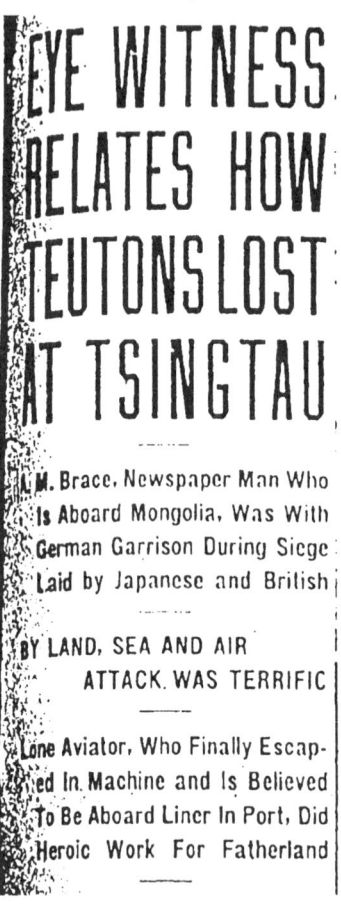

**EYE WITNESS RELATES HOW TEUTONS LOST AT TSINGTAU**

M. Brace, Newspaper Man Who Is Aboard Mongolia, Was With German Garrison During Siege Laid by Japanese and British

BY LAND, SEA AND AIR ATTACK. WAS TERRIFIC

Lone Aviator, Who Finally Escaped In Machine and Is Believed To Be Aboard Liner In Port, Did Heroic Work For Fatherland

"An eye witness of the events preceding and leading up to the capture of Tsingtau and the actual taking of the city by the Allied Japanese and British forces on November 6 arrived in Honolulu last evening on the Pacific Mail steamer Mongolia in the person of A.M Brace a reporter on the China Press, who was present in the doomed city as the representative of the Associated Press.

There was a full 2 1/2 column account of the Siege. The story continues from Page One.

## GENERAL KAMIO TAKES NO STOCK IN AERO WARSHIPS

Conqueror of Tsingtau and Governor of Kiao-Chau Has Poor Opinion of Airships

Scoffs At Stories That Aviators Are Doing Great Work With Their Bombs

## SPECTACULAR AERIAL ATTACK

"Mr. Brace said that the Japanese had eight naval airships constantly at work at throwing bombs into the city and reconnoitering... They dropped more than 200 bombs, with practically no military effect, although they fired and destroyed the polo club and some other non-military buildings."

## DARING GERMAN AVIATOR

"Gunther Plüschow, a German naval officer, was the sole

German means of reconnaissance during the land attack by the Allies' forces. One observation balloon sent up was fired upon and no longer used but the German aviator made daily trips aloft and was shot at and shrapneled many times without effect, and on one occasion had a revolver duel with a Japanese aviator whose machine was below him. Neither was hurt."

"Mr. Brace said the allied forces, particularly the British, had the greatest respect for Lieutenant Plüschow, who picked out the white tents of the British from the Japanese khaki some distance away from Tsingtau and bombarded them with home-made bombs made from coffee cans, dynamite and nails, but doing little damage".

## AIRMAN ESCAPES; ABOARD MONGOLIA

"After the surrender, Mr Brace said, he interviewed Lieutenant General Kamio, the Japanese commander, who told him the small damage inflicted by the Japanese aviators confirmed his own estimates, and said he had always taken with a grain of salt, the reports of the naval aviators regarding the damage they were inflicting."

"It is of particular interest to note that when the surrender was inevitable and but a few hours away, the German aviator flew away from Tsingtau on his monoplane and was supposed to have landed in Chinese territory and to have been interned. That was the last Mr. Brace had heard of him, but there was a story among the passengers on the Mongolia that "E.F. McGarvin," one of the passengers was none other than the daring German officer. The Associated Press man was unable to confirm the report."

The purpose for the apparent subterfuge is unclear as there is a photo of Brace and "Mr. McGarvin" together aboard ship. Plüschow writes that "they had swapped experiences of the Siege."

This curious newspaper item was also on the first page next to the Tsingtau account.

# JAPANESE AMBASSADOR DEPLORES TALK OF WAR

(Associated Press by Federal Wireless)

SCRANTON, Pennsylvania, December 23—Japanese Ambassador Chinda, in a speech made at a banquet here last night, deplored all stories of the possibility of a war between Japan and the United States. His speech was received with tumultuous applause and he was heartily cheered.

When Plüschow landed in San Francisco, after leaving Honolulu, he might have obtained money from Brace for a newspaper story or from the German Consulate. He did sell a story under his own byline to Sunset Magazine, San Francisco. It was printed in March 1915 titled "Flying Under Fire." It was written by him in English.

With single-mindedness of purpose Plüschow travelled to New York where he again changed his identity and papers. As Ernst Suse, a Swiss locksmith returning to his native land, he embarked on the Italian steamer Duca-degli Abruzzi bound for Naples in an attempt to reach Germany. But Plüschow, even with his near perfect identity papers, was captured at Gibraltar by the British when the ship curiously made an unscheduled stop.

He was sent to Donington Hall in England near Derby. The 17th Century manor house and its heavily guarded barbed-wired grounds had been converted into a prisoner-of-war camp for German officers.

Meanwhile, the only other German who escaped from Tsingtau

181

arrived in America. In 1915, the newspaper Post Dispatch reported a lecturer in St. Louis:

BAVARIAN TELLS HERE OF ESCAPE FROM TSINGTAU

"Otto Wiesinger says he fled disguised as Chinese after surrender to Japanese. He walked 225 miles. Then returned to Shanghai, where he previously was an importer, and thence to the United States aboard an American ship."

(The newspaper item continues)

"In fluent German, the Japanese officers," he said, "told me that, when Japan decides to make war on the United States, the first the United States will hear of it will be  news of the seizure of the Philippines and Hawaii."

That published statement was made twenty-seven years, almost to the month, BEFORE PEARL HARBOR!

Translated from a German newspaper editorial sometime during 1915 was also the following:

"And the day will come when Germany will recapture its magnificent possession... Tsingtau."

With these words, Mr. Otto Wiesinger from Shanghai closed his presentation of Tsingtau which he had enriched with slides." [The newspaper editorial continued]:

"May he be right! May he be one of those prophets who are respected in their own country. Tsingtau! The whole terrible tragedy of war lies in this name. The accursed British chose as their allies a race whose epithet is "the yellow peril." This yellow peril kindled by the British found its first rich bite in Tsingtau and will again look for another domain.

Videant Consules! May one watch out in this country for little yellow associates of the British which are so pampered by America. May fate spare America of a "Tsingtau!"

*****

Once again Plüschow made a daring escape. He was one of the few Germans ever to escape the famed British prisoner-of-war camp at Donington. The date was July 4, 1915. The London Daily Mail published this Extra Late War Edition.

# EXTRA LATE WAR EDITION

## HUNT FOR ESCAPED GERMAN,

### HIGH-PITCHED VOICE AS A CLUE.

Scotland Yard last night issued the following amended description of Gunther Pluschow, one of the two German prisoners who escaped from Doninston Hall, Leicestershire, on Monday :—

Height, 5ft. 8½in.; weight, 135lb.; complexion, fair; hair, blonde; eyes, blue; and tattoo marks, Chinese dragon on left arm.

As already stated in "The Daily Chronicle," Pluschow's companion, Trepplts; was recaptured on Monday evening at Millwall Docks. Both men are naval officers. An earlier description stated that Pluschow is 29 years old. His voice is high-pitched.

He is particularly smart and dapper in appearance, has very good teeth, which he shows somewhat prominently when talking or smiling; is "very English in manner," and knows this country well. He also knows Japan well. He is quick and alert, both mentally and physically, and speaks French and English fluently and accurately. He was dressed in a grey lounge suit or grey and yellow mixture suit.

London newspapers again published further accounts.
PLÜSCHOW STILL FREE
THE CHINESE DRAGON CLUE

———

Gunther Plüschow, the German naval Lieutenant, fugitive from Donington Hall has now been at large seven days. The Chinese dragon tattooed on his left arm while on service in the East should, however, betray his identity.

Further particulars of the escape with Lieutenant Treppitz, who was caught at Millwall Docks within twenty- four hours, show that last Sunday evening a violent thunderstorm raged over Donington Hall when the evening roll-call was taken. Instead of assembling with the other prisoners within the inner of the two rings of wire entanglement, the two hid within the outer circle. Their names were answered by other prisoners. A wooden plank near the outer ring showed how they got across the barbed wire.

———

Even yet another newspaper report:
MUCH ESCAPED FUGITIVE

———

PLÜSCHOW'S AEROPLANE FLIGHT FROM TSING-TAO.

———

"By the Chinese Dragon clue the authorities still hope to trace Lieutenant Gunther Plüschow, of the German Navy, who escaped from Donington Hall on Monday. The dragon is tattooed on the fugitive's left arm in Oriental colours. It was probably worked by a native artist, for although but 29 years of age, Plüschow has had an adventurous career in the Kaiser's Navy.

He was in Tsing-tao when the British and Japanese besieged that German fortress. Shortly before it fell Plüschow escaped in an aeroplane and some weeks later he was found on board a Japanese trading ship at Gibraltar."

NOTE; EVEN THEN NEWSPAPERS GAVE THE WRONG INFORMATION. Plüschow was aboard an Italian ship NOT Japanese!

"He will probably endeavour to sign on as a seaman in a neutral ship sailing from a British port, and, with this in view, a very careful watch is being kept at all ports throughout the country. Plüschow is a typical sailor, about 5ft. 6in. in height, with fair hair and fresh complexion. He would pass for a Dutchman with his broken English."

NOTE; HE SPOKE EXCELLENT ENGLISH AND FRENCH. THE ENGLISH NEWSPAPERS CONTRADICTED THEMSELVES EVEN THEN.

"Nothing he can do can remove the Chinese Dragon from his left arm, and his recapture should be but a matter of time."

———

Since Plüschow had no identification papers, he had the presence of mind to cut out and save several of the newspaper accounts.

His earlier intelligence gathering mission in London before the war came in handy. Plüschow spoke English and French as well as knowing the locale and British mores. Disguised as a union dockworker, he spent many harrowing days hiding out along the waterfront looking for a vessel in which to escape England. He was nearly recruited into the British army. Finally locating a Dutch ship ready to sail he swam to it with his clothes on his head and climbed aboard as a stowaway. When in Holland a sympathic secret service official did not detain him.

However, when arriving in Germany, Plüschow was given a mixed reception. World War One was nearly stalemated in France and Belgium with both Germany and the Allies dug into trench warfare. Espionage on both sides was rampant. At the frontier he was arrested by his own countrymen as a spy until he identified himelf by presenting the English newspaper descriptions. The officials were still not convinced. Then Plüschow dramatically rolled up his left sleeve and exhibited the dragon tattoo. With his identity proven, "The Flyer from Tsingtau", became well known. He was soon awarded the Royal Order of Hohenzollern and the Iron Cross, First Class by the Emperor. Later he received the Iron Cross Second Class and the Imperial Pilot's Shield and the Imperial Flying Cross that were both fashioned in gold.

He was also promoted to "Kapitanleutnant" and assigned as commanding officer of the Imperial German Naval Air Force Base at Libau near Riga, Latvia for the duration of the war. Plüschow was also to be awarded the "Blue Max", Germany's highest decoration, but the Kaiser abdicated before signing the orders.

It was here in Libau that he married in 1916. Gunther Plüschow and his wife Isot had one son who was born nearly two months before the Armistice was signed that ended World War One on November 11, 1918; four years after the fall of Tsingtau. The boy was given the first name of Guntolf which became his middle name after his father died and he inherited his father's name.

Plüschow's adventures did not end with the war. In 1924 he learned motion picture techniques from some famous German film makers and in 1925 he shipped aboard the full-rigged German sailing ship *Parma*. During the trip, he filmed a documentary of the ship's rough voyage from Chili to Germany around Cape Horn. That's when he became fascinated with the mysterious volcanic southern end of South America called the "Land of Fire," a little-known region with geysers not unlike Yellowstone Park.

In 1927 Plüschow acquired a vessel for an expedition to Tierra del Fuego at the tip of South America. The venture was financed by the Ullstein publishing house in Berlin. The 39 ton two-masted motor-sailor was 52 feet (16 meters) in length with a 16 foot (5 meters) beam. Besides sails it had a 50 horsepower diesel engine to get it through the doldrums. The vessel was built by the Busumer Shipbuilding Company and was named "Feuerland" after the "Land of Fire."

Plüschow as Captain of the five man crew, documented the 9,200 mile (14,300 km) voyage with a hand-cranked 35 mm motion picture camera. They reached the Chilean town of Punta Arenas in the Straits of Magellan where an important cargo had arrived by freighter; an open cockpit Heinkel HD 24 bi-plane equipped with floats. It had been assembled in an unused slaughter house by Plüschow's associate Ernst Drablow. The plane's name was prominently printed on the fuselage; "TSINGTAU".

This was the first aircraft in history to fly the desolate volcanic region over Chile and Argentina. For two years Plüschow, with his associate explored the uncharted southern tip of the Americas by sea and air. He filmed and photographed the glaciers and fiords which was later used by cartographers of both governments of Chile and Argentina.

However financial problems forced them to sell the boat and to live ashore in tents under the most difficult of conditions. Sixty three years later in 1993, the sturdy vessel is still being used as a fishing boat in the Faulkland Islands.

Landing amongst the floating ice was particularly hazardous as documented by the primitive motion picture camera. On January 28, 1931 Plüschow and his assistant had engine trouble and crashed into the Rio Brazzo near what is now Ushuaia, the southern most town in South America. The bodies were retrieved six hours later and after photos were taken, they were hurriedly buried to protect the remains from foxes and other scavangers. Gunther Plüschow, born February

8, 1886 was not quite forty five. This adventurer is even today remembered by the Argentineans. In 1991, a bicentenial memorial ceremony was held and documented by a German televison crew. A large bronze plaque cemented on a rocky cairn commemorates the site. The son of the pioneer aviator, who was only 13 when his father died, attended the ceremonies with his wife Rosemarie. His mother, Isot Plüschow, the wife of the flyer, had died in 1979 at the age of 90 in Berlin.

Gunter Guntolf Plueschow II (new spelling), now a Canadian citizen living in Winnipeg Canada, has been most helpful in providing documents, pictures and showing historic movie film to this writer.

Interesting documents revealed that the ancestors of this family can be traced back over 950 years to the House of Heinrich of Löwen (Lion) 1030 A.D. The lineage of Royal German ancestors from the province of Mecklenburg has now passed down through the aviator's one son to two grandsons and two great-grand children, albeit all Canadians.

*******

The "Dragon Master", or "The Kaiser's One-Man Air Force" (in Tsingtau, China) acquired a notable list of achievements in just 25 years between age 20 when becoming a naval cadet-officer to age 45 when he died...

* Imperial German Naval officer, world traveller, espionage/ intelligence agent;

* Pioneer Naval airman flying a primitive Rumpler-Taube became the World altitude record holder with Linnegogel (March 1914);

* Possibly history's first to engage in air-to-air combat against

Japanese aircraft over Tsingtau, downing one;

* Escaped, under orders, from Tsingtau before it surrendered;

* Escaped from Chinese internment in Nanking;

* Escaped from P.O.W. camp in England;

* Decorated by the Kaiser with the Hohenzollern Order and the Iron Cross, First Class and Second Class.

* Commanding Officer of the Imperial German Naval Air Force Base in Libau;

* Fathered a son to continue nearly a thousand years of lineage;

* Author of several German non-fiction books;

* "Square-rigger" sailor rounding Cape Horn;

* Motion picture documentary cameraman;

* Small boat adventurer, sailing 9,200 miles to Cape Horn;

* First to fly over and film uncharted Tierra del Fuego.

*****

Plüschow wrote these poignant words in English which were published in the San Franscisco Sunset Magazine in March 1915. They could be his epitaph:

"Like a great many officers of the German navy, I am a fatalist. I believe that when my time comes it matters little whether I am a mile in the air or in front of one of these fast American trams or, as you call them, street cars.

I love the zest of flying high in the blue sky with the rush of the wind about me, my Taube rocking and dipping but answering my slightest move.

I cannot help shouting at times when I look down at the map of mountains and rivers and sea beneath and realize how free and independent of all these things I am."

## THE END

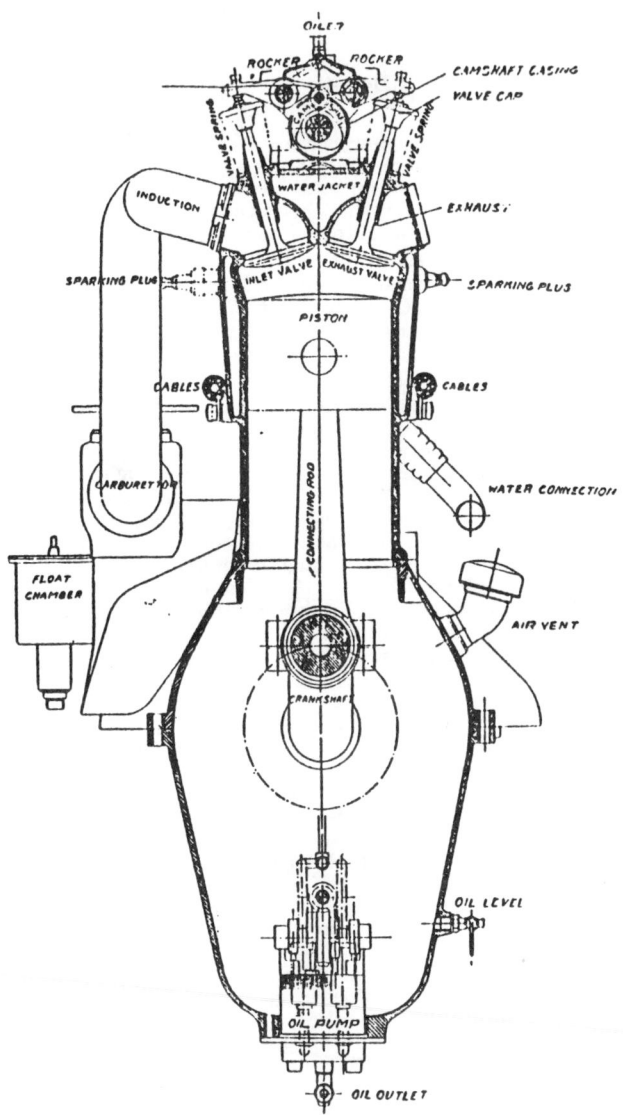

100-H.P. MERCEDES; SIDE SECTION

MERCEDES. (*Milnes-Daimler-Mercedes, Ltd.*, 132, *Long Acre, W.C.*)

There can surely be few cases on record of any single motor meeting with such remarkable and universal success as the Mercedes. It is no exaggeration to state that to all intents and purposes it has been the making of German aviation. To the best of our knowledge it holds every German record ; it certainly has to its credit the present world's duration record, set up by Ingold with 16 hours 20 minutes continuous flying. Its wonderful success is probably to be ascribed chiefly to its rigid adherence to the standard type of design ; in every respect it follows accepted standards ; to this, to the fine quality of the materials employed, and to the high degree of standardisation attained owing to the enormous output of the firm, its reliability is mainly due. .

It consists of 6 cylinders, cast in pairs with ordinary copper water-jackets. The hot water is led to a water-jacket surrounding the carburettor, which is further warmed by hot air. The overhead valves are operated by a gear-driven overhead camshaft completely enclosed in a casing. Two sparking plugs are fitted to each cylinder and two magnetos are provided, giving highly efficient combustion and eliminating motor troubles owing to magneto defects. Two carburettors are also fitted, each supplying three cylinders ; they form an integral part of the upper half of the crankcase.

Lubrication is by forced feed through a double piston pump. The base of the crankcase constitutes the oil reservoir, and contains a sufficient supply for a six hours' run. Pressure in the tanks is obtained from the exhaust.

All the working parts of the engine are situated on one side, rendering adjustment an easy matter.

The bore of the 100-H.P. Mercedes is 120 mm. with a stroke of 140 mm. It develops from 95-H.P. at 1,200 r.p.m. to a full 105-H.P. at 1,350 r.p.m. The weight of the engine complete, but without radiator, is only 410 lb., which works out at the remarkably low figure of under 4 lb. per H.P. Its fuel consumption is under 7 gallons per hour, its oil consumption negligible—a good deal less than half a gallon an hour, to be precise.

A Bosch magneto self-starter is a standard fitting, and a most useful one, since it never fails provided the cylinders are doped and there is some compression.

# AUTHOR'S POST SCRIPT:

I wish to thank Gunter Plueschow, not only for permission to publish the English translated quotations of his father, the pictures, and other works which is owned by him, but the hospitality and encouragement given me by Gunter and his wife Rosemarie during my visit and research.

During my tape recorded interview, I learned that the son's background is as adventurous as his father... known as "The Dragon Master of Tsingtau"... but that is another story.

******

## SOURCES

* Shnenshi shitsu, Defense Agency, Tokyo
* National Archives, Washington, DC
* Library of Congress, Washington, DC
* United States Naval Institute, Annapolis, MD
* Hoover Institution, Stanford, CA
* Library of Contempory History, Stuttgart, Germany
* Public Records Office, London
* Bundesarchiv-Militararchiv, Freiburg Germany
* U.S. Army Military Research Collection, Carlisle, Pennsylvania
* Experimental Aircraft Association Foundation-Boeing Aeronautical Library, Oshkosh, WI
* Hawaii State Library, Honolulu HI
* Carrel Morgan, Wayne, NJ
* Gunter Guntolf Plueschow, Winnipeg, Canada

# Bibliography

* Bowen, Ezra, "Knights of the Air," Time-Life Books 1980
* Canning, Craig Noel: "The Japanese Occupation of Shantung during World War 1" University of Ann Arbor, Mich. Microfilms 1979
* Godshall, Wilson L.; "Tsingtau Under Three Flags" Commercial Press, Shanghai, 1919.
* Gottberg, Otto von, "Die Helden von Tsingtau," Ullstein, Berlin, 1915.
* Henze, Karl G., "Pluschow uber Tsingtau, Flieger im Fernen Osten." Steiniger, Berlin 1941.
* Hoyt, Edwin P: "The Fall of Tsingtao," Barker; London 1975
* Jones, Jefferson, "The Fall of Tsingtau, With a Study of Japan's Ambitions in China." Houghton Mifflin Co. Boston-New York, 1915.
* Kennet, Lee, "The First Air War 1914-1918," The Free Press New York, NY.
* Kuechler, Kurt, "Die letzten Tage von Tsingtau." Heilbronn: Salzer 1916.
* Meyer-Waldeck, Vizeadmiral, "Das Schutzgebiet Kiautschou." In: Die Deutsche Flotte in grosser Zeit. 3.Aufl. Berlin 1916.
* Musciano, Walter A, "Eagles of the Black Cross," Obolensky, New York, 1965.
* Noffsinger, James P., "World War I Aviation Books in English: An Annotated Bibliography," pg.209 no.1154, Scarecrow Press, Metuchen, NJ & London, 1987.
* Norem, Ralph; "Kiaochow Leased Territory, University of Berkeley, CA, 1936
* Pluschow, Gunther, "Die Abenteuer des Fliegers von Tsingtau," Ullstein; Berlin, 1917.
* Schultze-Jena, Kurt, "Der Kampf um Tsingtau," Nossler & Co. Shanghai, 1915.
* Schrecker, John E., "Imperialism and Chinese Nationalism; Germany in Shangtung." Harvard University, Cambridge, Mass, 1971.
* Seneki Nichi-Doku: "Nichi-Doku Seneki kinen shasincho," Tokio, Japan, 1915
* Vollerthun, Waldemar: "Der Kampf um Tsingtau." Eine Episode aus dem Weltkrlieg 1914-1918 nagebuchblattern Hirzel; Leipzig, 1920
* Vortrag, Kurt: "Der Kampf um Tsingtau," Schultze,..Jena: Fischer 1916
* Wiesinger, Otto, "Als Kriegsfreiwilliger in Tsingtau." Nossler & Co. Shanghai, 1915
* Woodhead,H.G.W., "Adventures in Far Eastern Journalism; A Record of Thirty-Three Years Experience." Hokuseido Press, Tokyo, 1935.
* Wyrall, E., "The History of the Duke of Corwall's Light Infantry, 1914-1919," Methuen, London, 1932.

APPENDIX

# ARTICLES

* Jones, Clifford; "Japanese Landing at Tsingtao", Coast Artillery Journal, #2 1928

* Layman, R.D.; "Japanese Naval Aviation," United States Naval Proceedings (Sept 1973)

* Knox, E.F.; "The Siege of Tsing-Tao" The Journal of the United Service Institution of India, (XLIV) July 1915

* Morgan, Carrel B.; "An Ancient Taube Found in China" Popular Aviation June 1937 pg 38,66.

* "Naval Operations Against Tsingtau" Journal of the United States Artillery, May-June 1916

* Perry, Emil B.; "The Siege of Tsingtao", United States Naval Institute Proceedings, Vol 55 January-June 1929.

* Pluschow, Gunther, "Flying Under Fire," Sunset Magazine, San Francisco, March 1915.

* Zabecki, David T.; "Kaiser's Asian Sunset", Military History, vol 10 pgs 51-57 June 1993

## FURTHER READING;

"The Fall of Tsingtau." J. Jones; Houghton Mifflin Co. 1915
"German War Birds" Vigilant; London 1933
"They Fought For The Sky" Quentin Reynolds; Rinehart & Co 1957
"The Japanese Siege of Tsingtau" Charles Burdick. Archon. 1976
"Taube, Dove of War," Col.J.A. deVries, Historical Aviation, 1978

## ABOUT THE AUTHOR:

Robert E. Whittaker was born in Shanghai, China of American parents. Father; a textile engineer: Mother; a teacher and Associated Press correspondent.

Whittaker lived in Tsingtau for over 17 years, was familiar with the old German fortifications and knew several of the German veterans who had first-hand accounts of the siege.

He is a 1944 graduate of the U.S. Merchant Marine Academy, Kings Point, NY and a former merchant ship's Captain (Master Mariner) and Officer in the U.S. Naval Reserve. He has travelled 16 times around the world and visited over 86 countries.

He is an independent film and video WRITER/director/ cameraman who has credits on numerous military and documentary films and videos shot in the U.S. and abroad.

Whittaker's brief and only flying experience has been lessons in a Piper Cub which he soloed prior to his appointment as cadet-midshipman.

In addition to 47 film and video scripts, he has also written for a variety of magazines and newspapers in the U.S. and as contributing editor to the Free China Journal in Taiwan. Under the pseudonym of "Lao Wei" he has written and edited a published Compass Book of ancient and modern International proverbs and sayings.

Whittaker is completing a historical novel based in Japan and China from 1912 to 1989. He has three grown children, is married for the 2nd time and presently living in Cleveland, Wisconsin near Lake Michigan.

INDEX

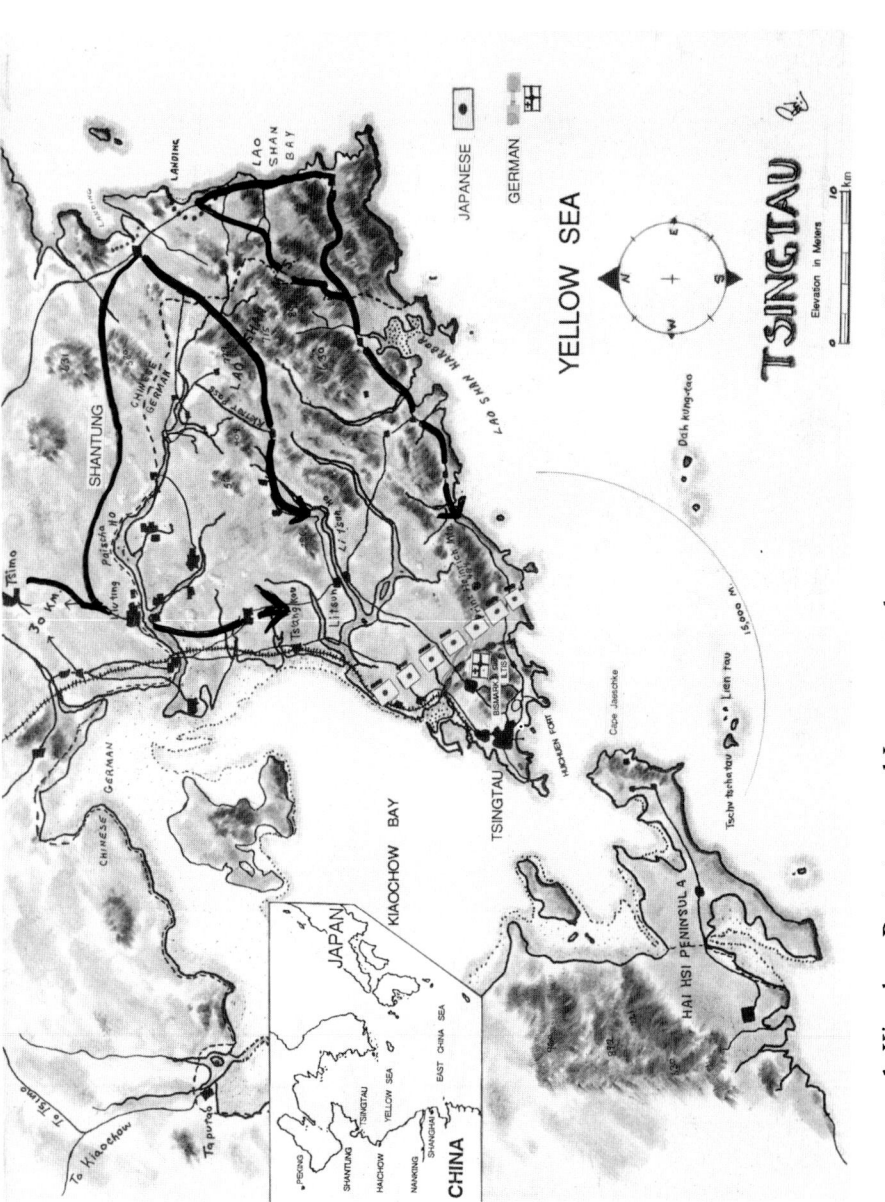

1. Kiaochow Protectorate and Japanese attack routes          (drawn by R. Whittaker)

206

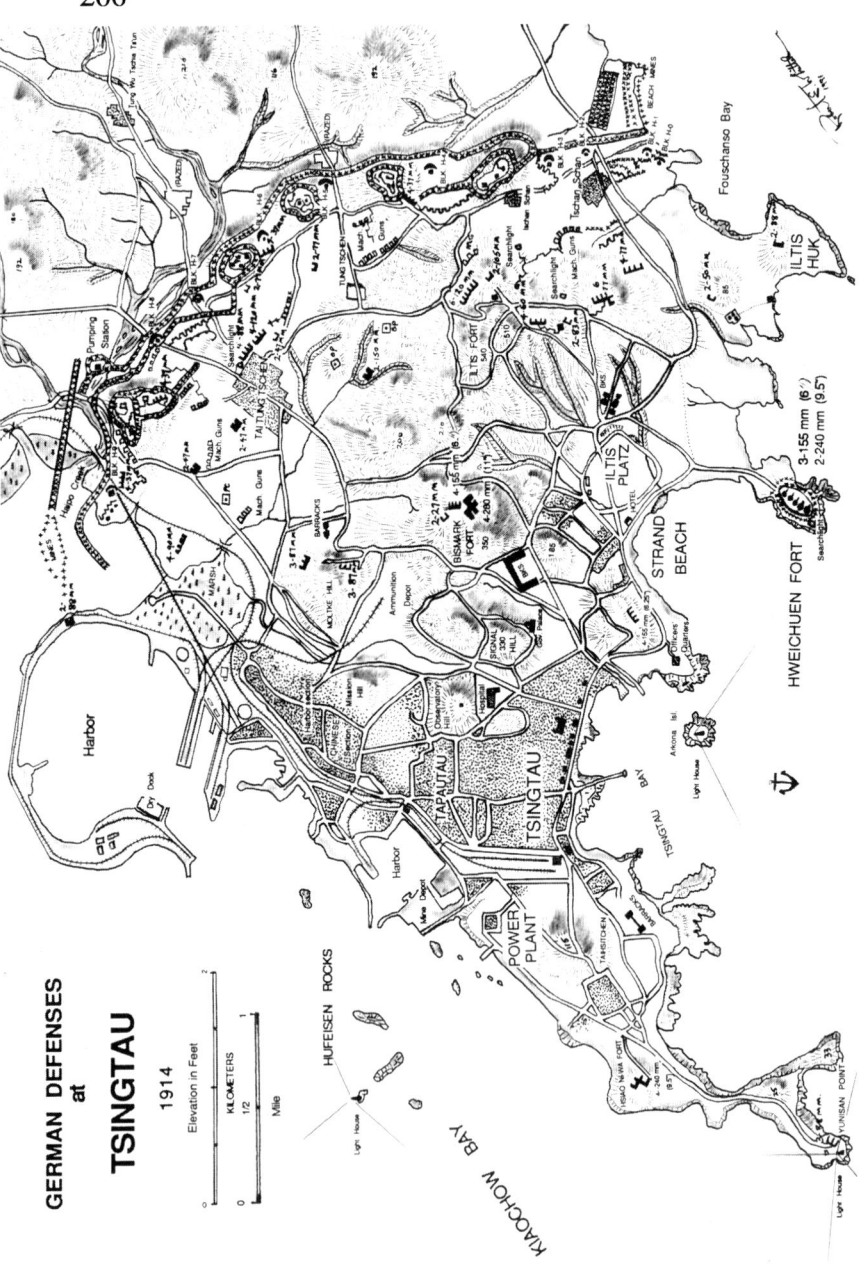

2. Tsingtau & fortifications. Redrawn and enhanced from a German battle "Plan".  (drawn by R. Whittaker)

3. Captain Alfred von Meyer-Waldeck, Governor of Kiaochow and Commander-In-Chief of the German forces.

Album von Tsingtau, Jefferson Jones Collection
Hoover Institution Archives

4. The Governor's "castle".

5. Government Haus. German administration building.

Album von Tsingtau, Jefferson Jones Collection — Hoover Institution Archives

6. Kaiser Wilhelm Strasse fronting Tsingtau Bay. German-Chinese high school to the right. The Governor's mansion to the left. Signal Hill and antennae beyond Christ Church and Government Haus.

Album von Tsingtau, Jefferson Jones Collection —Hoover Institution Archives

7. Tsingtau Bay looking south. Christ Church to the left. Beyond is the officer's house. Arkona (Green Island) center and Government Haus to the right.

Album von Tsingtau, Jefferson Jones Collection — Hoover Institution Archives

8. Post & Telegraph office. The empty streets were partially due to the cameras' slow shutter speed that turned the pedestrians crossing the street into ghost images.

Album von Tsingtau, Jefferson Jones Collection
Hoover Institution Archives

9. Albert Strasse. Typical European residences in a park-like setting.

Album von Tsingtau, Jefferson Jones Collection
Hoover Institution Archives

10. Prince Heinrich Mt. (Eagles Nest) looking north-east from Iltis Huk.
courtesy — Nancy Allman Burnham

11. From Laoshan looking south-west towards Tsingtau. Hweichuen Fort is the point of land, 30 km (18.6 miles) in the distant background.
unknown photographer

12. Typical Chinese village near Lao Shan (Old Mountain)

13. Strand Hotel situated between the bathing beach and "airfield" at Iltis Platz.

Album von Tsingtau, Jefferson Jones Collection
Hoover Institution Archives

15. III Seebatalion (Marines) in parade uniforms.
Bundesarchiv-Militararchiv

14. Typical German cavalry officer of the "Mountain Navy Horsemen."
Album von Tsingtau, Jefferson Jones Collection
Hoover Institution Archives

16. Hweichuen Fort; 3 Krupp 155 mm guns and the author's father and mother, 1917.

Robert Whittaker

17. Hweichuen Fort looking south; 2-240 mm guns. The author, his mother and Japanese nurse-maid.

Robert Whittaker

18. The Big Harbor, taken by Takahashi which surreptitiously include German warships.
Takahashi — Hoover Institution Archives

218

19. Strand Beach as it would have looked with Plüschow's aircraft coming in over the hotel for a landing. This is the combination of a 1914 photo and 1994 technology through a digitized computer-integrated image of a seven inch scale-model of a Rumpler Taube (Dove).

Robert Whittaker, Anthony J. Kashinn

20. Tsingtau beach "Number One" 80 years later in 1993. Strand Hotel still exists to the left.

Robert Whittaker

21. "A Ship of the Sky". A scale model of the Rumpler Taube. It was built "from scratch" in 184 hours (23 eight hour days).

built & photographed by Robert Whittaker

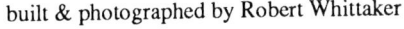

22. A model of the Rumpler Taube.

built & photographed by Robert Whittaker

220

23. The airfield at Iltis Platz after Plüschow's first flight. (As it would have looked) Digital-Computer Integration.

Robert Whittaker, Anthony J. Kashinn

24. Lt. Plüschow in his Rumpler Taube

Plüschow

25. Cockpit of the Taube

Plüschow

26. Model of a Rumpler Taube

Robert E. Whittaker

27. Plüschow's crashed Taube

G. Plüschow

28. The Japanese flagship *Suwo* and cruisers *Tango* and *Iwami*.

Hoover Institution Archives

224

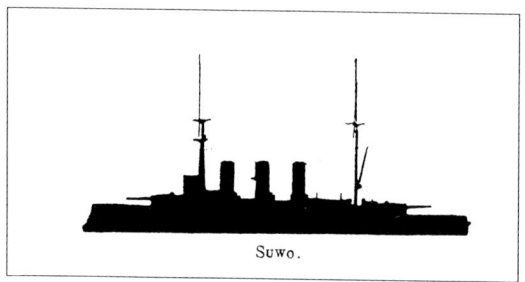

Suwo.

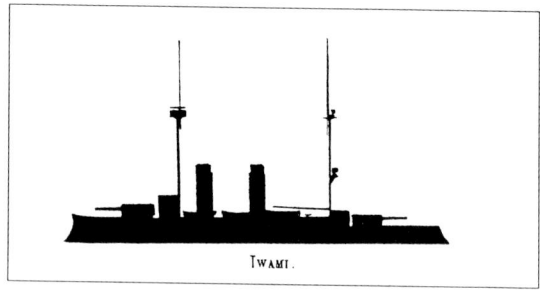

Iwami.

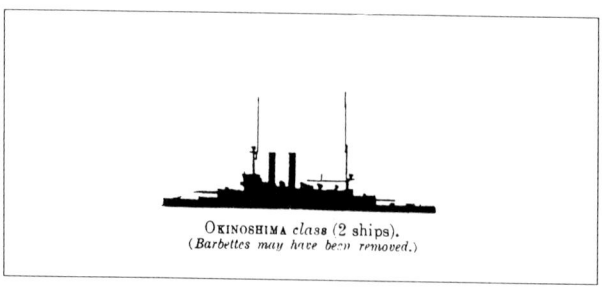

Okinoshima class (2 ships).
(Barbettes may have been removed.)

29. Identity silhouettes of *Suwo, Iwami* and *Okinoshima*. Only a small part of the blockading Japanese fleet. (1" = 160ft)

Jane-1914

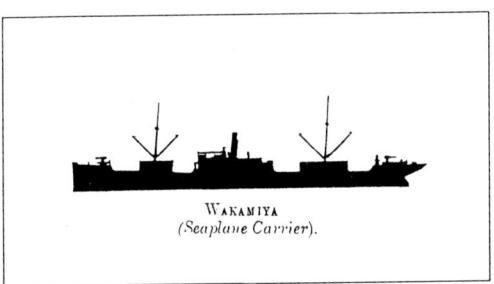

30. A Maurice Farman float plane being off-loaded from the Japanese "mother ship".

60 Years of Japanese Aviation

WAKAMIYA
(Seaplane Carrier).

31. Recognition silhouette of *Wakamiya Maru* "the first aircraft carrier used in combat." (1" = 160ft)

Jane-1914

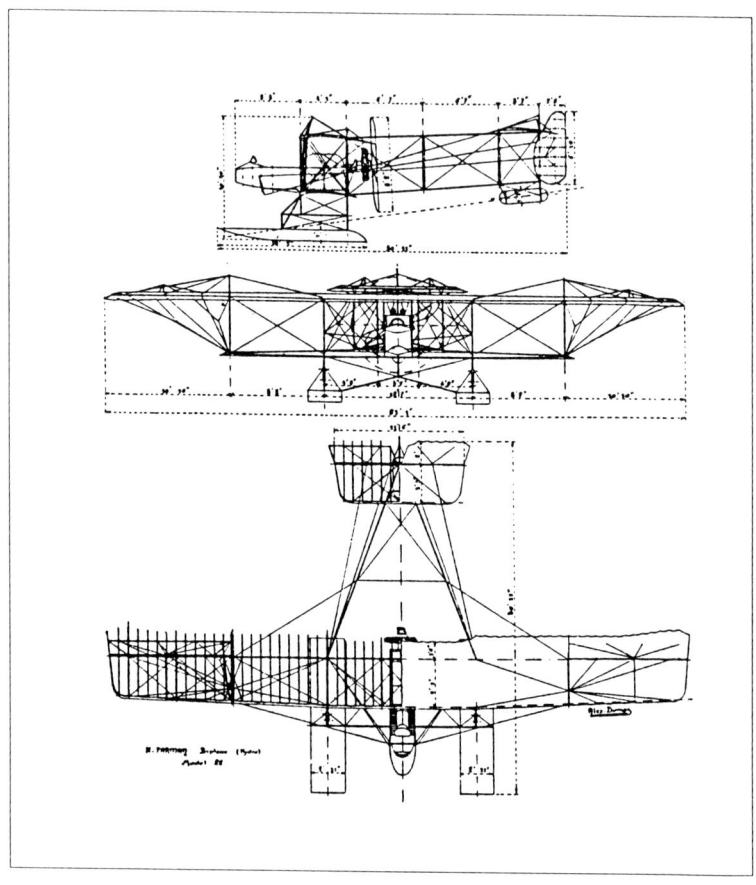

32. Schematics of the Maurice Farman sea plane.

"The workmanship as usual is above reproach. Built-up wooden struts are used throughout, and an interesting point is that all the metal fittings below the bottom plane were of brass throughout to prevent corrosion. Both front and rear extremities of the floats are sprung by rubber cord."

Aeronautics; Jan 1914.

33. Maurice Farman alongside "mother ship" preparing
for take off.

60 Years of Japanese Aviation

INSIGNIA OF RANK ON SLEEVES FOR EXECUTIVES.

Gross-Admiral (= Admiral of the Fleet) as Admiral but 4 upper stripes.

**Crowns may have been removed.**

| Admiral. | Vize-Admiral. (Vice-Ad.) | Kontre-Admiral. (Rear-Ad.) | Komnodore (Commodore). | Kapitän zu See (Captain) | Fregatten-Kapitän & Kapitän zu See. Korvetten-Kapitän. (Commander) | Kapitän-Leutnant. (Lieut.-Comm.) | Oberleut z. See (Lieut.) | Leutenant z. See (Sub-Lieut.) |

Flaggoffiziere.    Stabsoffiziere.    Subalternoffiziere.

34. Sleeve insignias of rank; German Navy

INSIGNIA OF RANK—EXECUTIVE OFFICERS—SLEEVES.    (Changed to this; 1908).

| Executive Branch: Corresponding British or U.S.: | Tai-sho. *Admiral* | Chu-sho. *Vice-Ad.* | Sho-sho. *Rear-Ad.* | Tai-sa. *Captain.* | Chu-sa. *Commander.* | Sho-sa. *Lieut. Com.* | Tai-i. *Lieutenant.* | Chu-i. *Sub-Lieut.* | Sho-i *Acting Sub-Lieut.* | Sho-i Ko-hoshei. *Midshipman.* |
| | | | | | | | | | | Has a stripe half the width of a Sho-i. |

35. Sleeve insignias of rank; Japanese Navy

37. Landing site near Lao Shan. The token forces of British were surprised to see the Union Jack and the Rising Sun flags. That was the extent of real cooperation between the two Allies.

Public Record Office, London

36. Lieutenant General Mitsuomi Kamio, Japanese Siege Commander

Hoover Institution Archives

39. Typical British soldier. Winter clothing and full rations did not arrive until several weeks later.

Hoover Institution Archives

38. Typical Japanese soldier. The Arisaka Type 38, 6.5mm light-recoil weapon was adopted for the short-statured troops.

Hoover Institution Archives

40. Japanese 280mm howitzer. Called "Ginger Beer Bottles" by the British, there were over 140 of these 11 inch guns.

National Archives

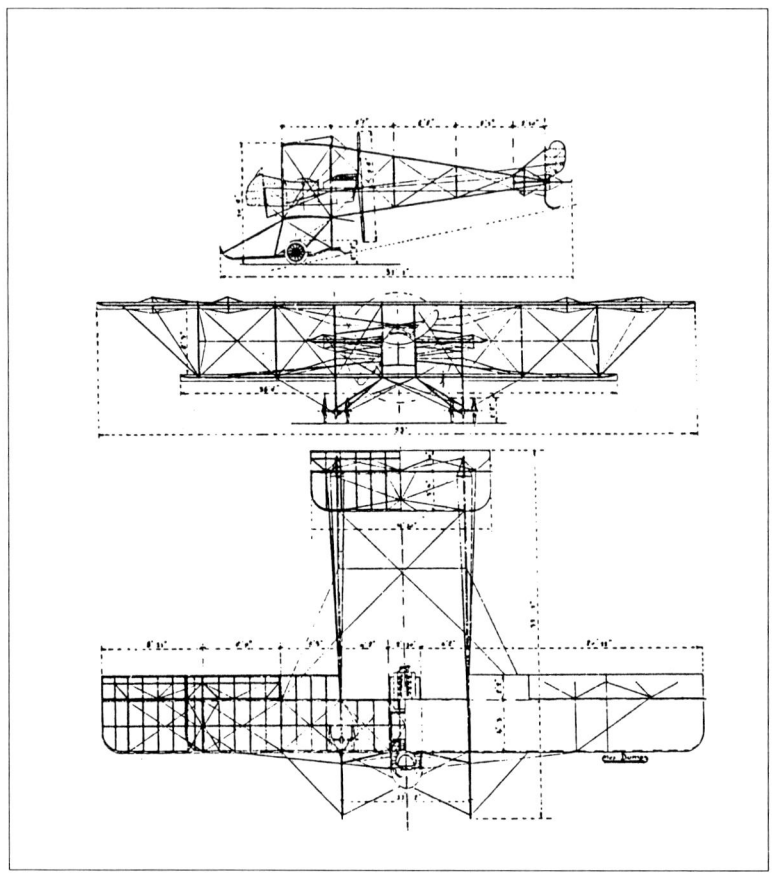

41. Schematic of the Maurice Farman land plane. They were copied and built by the Japanese. Designated Type "Fu".

60 Years of Japanese Aviation

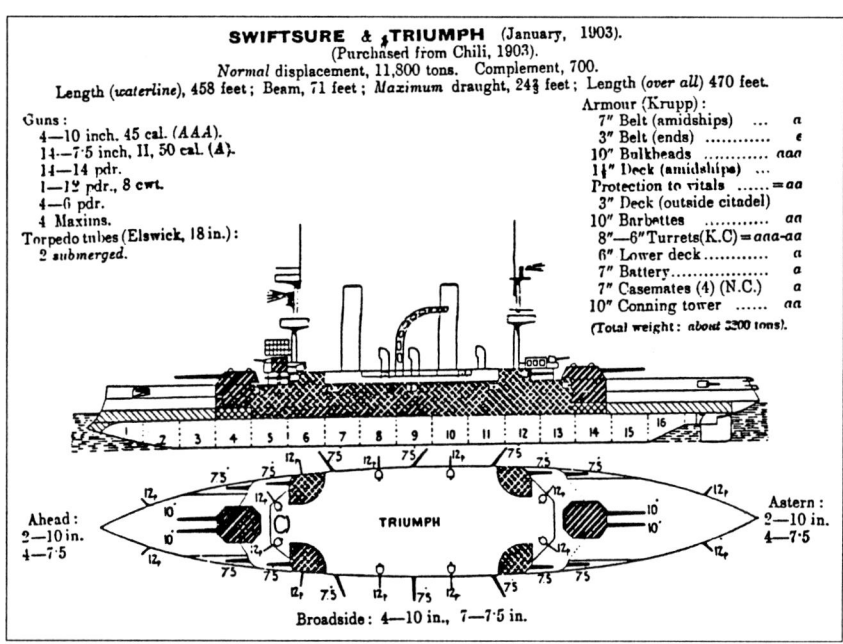

42. H.M.S. *Triumph*

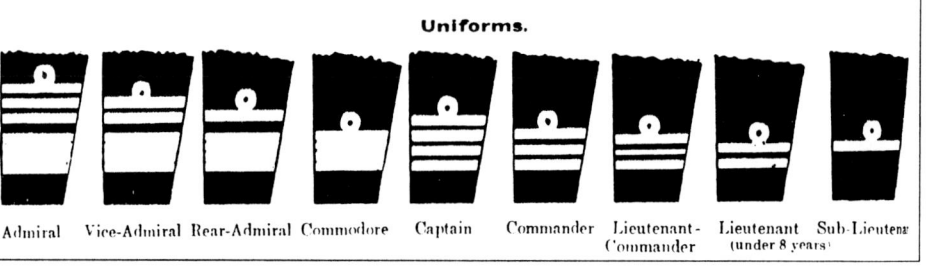

43. Sleeve insignias of British Naval officers.

44. *Kaiserin Elizabeth*; Austrian Cruiser

Jane-1914

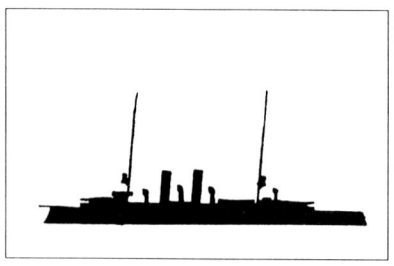

*Kaiserin Elizabeth* (1" = 160ft)

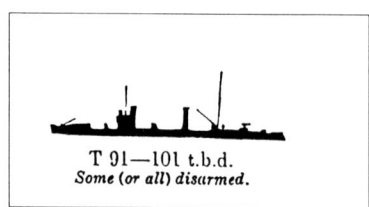

45. Recognition silhouette of the German
torpedo-boat S-90 (1" = 160ft)

46. Japanese cavalry charge. These illustrations were made during the siege and circulated in Japan in lieu of classified and not so dramatic photographs.

Hoover Institution Archives

236

47. Japanese attacking Shatze-kou. Dramatized and exaggerated.
Hoover Institution Archives

48. Japanese navy 3-man float plane bombing Tsingtau. The illustration of the bay was based on a Takahashi post card and other photographs.

Hoover Institution Archives

238

49. Captured Germans from the Haipo water-works.
Jefferson Jones Collection, Hoover Institution Archives

50. Captured Germans and their guards.
Bundesarchiv-Militararchiv

51. British troops marching into Tsingtau, preceding the Japanese victory parade by days.

Jefferson Jones Collection, Hoover Institution Archives

52. German gun battery self-destroyed.

"It affords an example of the thoroughness of German destructive methods. Only scrap metal are left of the solidly framed gun-mountings, gun-carriages and elaborate mechanical gear."

Photo by G.P.U. 1914, Office of Naval Intelligence

53. German Torpedo-boat *S-90* self-destroyed and beached in neutral China 60 miles south of Tsingtau.

unknown Japanese photographer

54. A 21 centimeter 6 ton Krupp Siege-Howitzer blown up by the Germans before surrender. "According to the laws of war, a beaten antagonist is empowered before surrendering to destroy all Government property and war-material in his possession in order that it may not be of use to the enemy."

Photo by G.P.U. 1914, Office of Naval Intelligence

55. Japanese victory parade. Note the Japanese flags held by German non-combatants. Aircraft were always in these scenes.

Hoover Institution Archives

56. Plüschow's Taube by the walled town of Haïchow.
Doctor Ruth Bennet Morgan

57. Plüschow by his wingless Taube with missionary children.
The Chinaman in the cockpit is a servant of the missionaries.

Doctor Ruth Bennet Morgan

Doctor Ruth Bennet Morgan

58. Rigging details of the Taube.

59. Plüschow presenting the plane's Mercedes engine to the Chinese Magistrate
Doctor Ruth Bennet Morgan

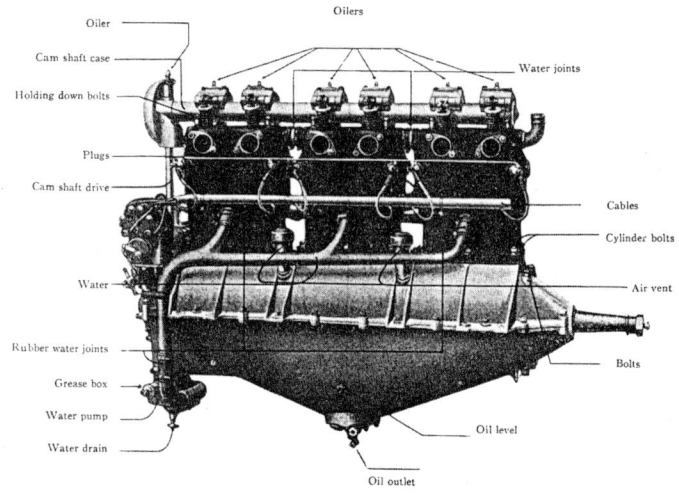

Oilers

Oiler

Cam shaft case

Holding down bolts

Water joints

Plugs

Cam shaft drive

Cables

Cylinder bolts

Water

Air vent

Rubber water joints

Grease box

Bolts

Water pump

Water drain

Oil level

Oil outlet

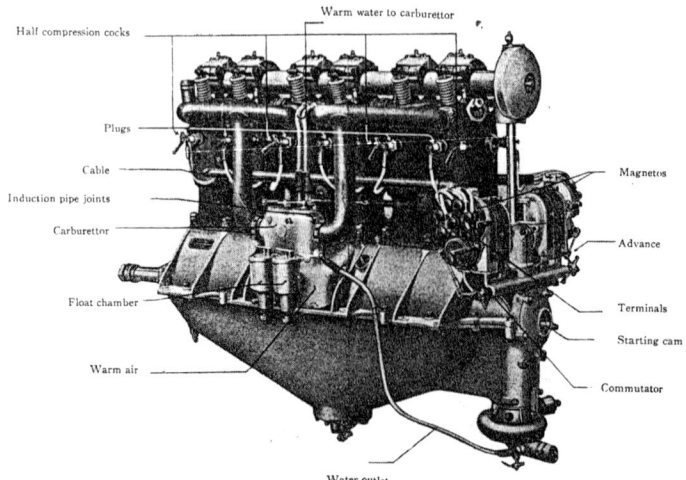

Warm water to carburettor

Half compression cocks

Plugs

Cable

Magnetos

Induction pipe joints

Carburettor

Advance

Float chamber

Terminals

Starting cam

Warm air

Commutator

Water outlet

THE 6-CYLINDER 100-H.P. MERCEDES ENGINE

60. The 6-cylinder 100-H.P. Mercedes Engine

61. Plüschow burning his plane at Haichow.

Doctor Ruth Morgan

62. Gunter G. Plueschow holding the picture of his father.

Robert Whittaker

63. Last known photo of the flyer Plüschow prior to his death. Note that the Heinkel HD-24 in the composite was named Tsingtau.

G. Plueschow

64. The author, holding the model of the Rumpler Taube and a piece of the wing fabric from Plüschow's Taube courtesy of Carrel Morgan

Robert & Nancy Whittaker